Data Rookies:
Data Wrangling Essentials

Clean, Transform, and Prepare Data

Published by
Data Analytics Curriculum
https://www.dataanalyticscurriculum.com

Supplements and Companion Books

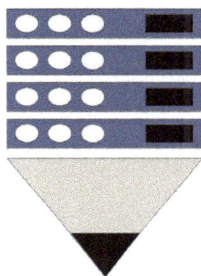

Data Analytics Curriculum

Data Analytics Curriculum, LLC develops approachable and visually engaging educational materials designed to make data science and technology accessible to learners ranging from high school through college and independent study.

The content texts, such as this book, are sold separately from the lab and exercise books because they can be paired with multiple technologies.

This book has accompanying lab exercise books available for R (coding-based) and Orange (non-coding-based), with plans to add more technologies in the future.

For additional titles, lab books, solution guides, slides, and other teaching and learning resources, please visit our store or website:

Website: https://www.dataanalyticscurriculum.com

Contents

Contents

Chapter 1

INTRODUCTION

1-1 Definition and Context

> **Learning Outcomes**
>
> **1-1-1** Define data analytics and explain its purpose.
> **1-1-2** Outline the steps involved in the data analytics workflow.
> **1-1-3** Explain the concept and importance of data wrangling.
> **1-1-4** Describe the three-step process of data wrangling.

Fundamentally, data analytics is the process of taking raw data and turning it into useful, actionable information. This involves the transformation of raw data into actionable insights, essentially extracting value from data for organizational benefit. To conceptualize this process, it is helpful to define the entire data analytics workflow into specific steps.

Obtain and import data ➡ Explore data ➡ Wrangle data ➡ Analyze data ⇨ Produce results

Data wrangling, the focal point of this book, plays a crucial role in preparing data for analysis. Although the workflow is depicted as a linear path, it often involves iterative steps rather than a straight linear process because often one must step back and revise things.

Data Analytics Workflow

Let's explore the steps of the data analytics workflow. The workflow typically encompasses obtaining and importing data, exploring data, wrangling data, analyzing data, and finally, producing results.

Obtain and import data

To initiate the workflow, the first step is obtaining and importing data from various sources, either locally or online.

Explore data

Subsequently, it's imperative to explore the data thoroughly to understand its contents and identify any issues. This process is often referred to as data profiling.

Wrangling data

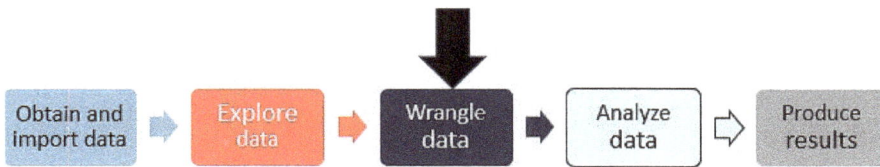

Wrangling the data involves preparing it for analysis by restructuring and cleaning it. The coming chapters in this book detail this process.

Analyze data

Once the data is prepared, the analysis phase commences, encompassing basic descriptive statistics, statistical modeling, and other advanced analytical techniques like unstructured text analysis and data mining.

Produce results

Finally, the results are produced, which stakeholders utilize for decision-making.

Purpose of Data Wrangling

Data wrangling involves ensuring data is in the correct form and clean for subsequent analytical processes. This is not merely about cleaning; it also entails restructuring and modifying data. While it's sometimes perceived as mundane work, it's a vital aspect of a data analyst's role.

Data wrangling can be conceptualized as a three-step process, which will serve as the structural framework for this entire book. The process involves cleaning, modifying, and restructuring data.

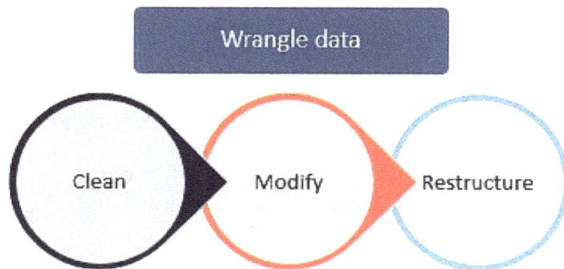

Cleaning entails addressing issues column by column, such as rectifying spelling errors or ensuring data consistency. Modification involves altering or transforming existing data, often to normalize units, join fields, or make other adjustments. Restructuring, on the other hand, entails reshaping or transforming data, which may involve sub setting, modifying layout, or creating summary datasets.

This book will adhere to this systematic approach, as illustrated in a simple diagram. This structured format provides a clear roadmap for learners to follow.

Example

Data wrangling plays a vital role in ensuring that raw data is ready for analysis. A good example of this comes from a nonprofit organization that conducted an online survey to understand community needs. The organization collected responses from over 2,000 participants. However, when the data was downloaded, it was messy and inconsistent. Location names were recorded in different ways ("NY," "New York," "N.Y."), dates were in mixed formats, and phone numbers were inconsistent.

As a data analyst, the first step was to obtain and import the data into tools like Excel and RStudio. Next, I explored the data through profiling to spot missing values, inconsistent text entries, and formatting issues. This exploration revealed that much of the data needed cleaning before any real analysis could take place.

The wrangling process began with cleaning the data by standardizing location names and fixing errors. Then, modifying the data involved unifying the date formats and splitting phone numbers into clear components. Finally, restructuring the data helped create a summary table showing how many respondents came from each state and what their primary needs were.

After wrangling, the data was ready for analysis. Descriptive statistics and cross-tabulations were used to find important patterns, such as the most commonly reported needs and how they varied by age group. The final results were presented in clear tables and graphs, which the nonprofit used to make decisions about how to allocate funding.

This case shows that without careful data wrangling, analyses could lead to incorrect or misleading conclusions. Proper preparation ensures that data is clean, consistent, and structured in a way that supports valid and actionable insights.

Review Questions

1. What is data analytics, and why is it important for organizations?
2. List and briefly describe the five main steps of the data analytics workflow.
3. Why is the data analytics workflow often described as iterative rather than strictly linear?
4. Define data wrangling. How does it differ from just "cleaning" data?
5. What are the three main steps involved in the data wrangling process? Provide an example of each.
6. Why is data wrangling considered a crucial part of a data analyst's work, even if it can seem mundane?

1-2 Tools and Professional Practice

Learning Outcomes

1-2-1 Identify coding and non-coding tools used in data wrangling.

1-2-2 Select the appropriate tool for data wrangling tasks.

1-2-3 Understand professional practices in project management, documentation, and ethics.

1-2-4 Recognize and explain the limitations of data wrangling tools and techniques.

1-2-5 Understand the importance of knowing the origin and legality of data.

1-2-6 Assess the reliability and quality of data based on its source and collection method.

Tools

A variety of tools and types of tools are used in data wrangling. Given the diverse nature of data analysis tasks, it's improbable for data analysts to rely on just one tool. Therefore, familiarity with various tools is essential. Typically, analysts may utilize spreadsheets, analysis programs, and programming languages depending on the task at hand. However, it's unnecessary to master redundant tools; instead, learners should focus on acquiring proficiency in a diverse yet efficient set of tools.

A prominent consideration in data analysis is whether to code or not. While programming skills have been emphasized in many analytics programs, their necessity may diminish with advancements in AI. Therefore, it's crucial to discern between coding and non-coding tools. Non-coding tools like Excel, OpenRefine, SPSS, Orange, and Tableau offer intuitive interfaces for data manipulation and analysis, catering to a wide range of analytical needs.

When considering the benefits of non-coding tools, one may wonder why we would invest time in coding when there are user-friendly point-and-click options available. However, the advantage of coding lies in its ability to reuse code for automating tasks, a capability not readily available in most non-coding tools.

Coding may still be necessary for certain novel tasks that may not be available in point and click software. Additionally, coding facilitates sharing, reproducing, and version control, although it does come with a steep learning curve.

Despite its advantages, coding may entail significant time investment in maintenance and updates, potentially negating its benefits. Moreover, with the rise of AI, the importance of programming skills may diminish over time. Python and R currently dominate the coding landscape as of this writing, but languages are always subject to change.

SAS, although overlooked in some contexts, remains prevalent in certain industries like pharmaceuticals and government. SQL, on the other hand, boasts ease of use and is commonly embedded in other languages. While emerging languages like Julia may offer alternatives, Python and R seem firmly established for the foreseeable future.

On the non-coding side, point-and-click software offers accessibility and ease of learning, with tools like Microsoft Excel being widely accessible. However, they often lack documentation of what processes have been implemented on the data, potentially hindering reproducibility. OpenRefine, a tool available as open source, bridges this gap by providing a user-friendly interface while maintaining documentation and reproducibility features.

Another drawback of point-and-click tools is their potential difficulty in handling very large datasets, where programming becomes advantageous. Manual repetition of tasks in point-and-click systems can be time-consuming, although some offer macros to aid in automation.

Professional Practices

While data wrangling is not yet a licensed profession, it's worth considering appropriate professional practices. Typically, professions are governed by professional organizations with guidelines and regulations, although this isn't the case for data analytics just yet. However, it's prudent to contemplate what constitutes appropriate professional conduct in this field.

Four key professional practices emerge: possessing project management skills, diligent documentation, adherence to applicable ethics and laws, and recognizing one's limitations.

Professional Practice

Project management

Project management skills entail competencies for planning, executing, and successfully completing projects. Certification programs offer accessible pathways to acquiring these skills, essential for career advancement in data analytics.

Documentation

Documentation is another crucial practice, vital for transparency, repro-ducibility, and collaboration. Comprehensive documentation ensures that activities, analysis plans, data sources, and modifications are recorded systematically, facilitating future reference and collaboration. It enables both self-reproducibility and reproducibility by others, enhancing trust and accountability in data analytics endeavors.

Data analyst at a minimum should document: - Source data and created datasets and where stored. - Dates work performed. - Names of datasets. - Activities performed on data. - Planned work to be done. - Software used.

Laws and ethics

Adherence to applicable ethics and laws is paramount, even in the absence of comprehensive regulations in the data analytics field. Upholding ethical standards and legal obligations fosters trust and integrity in data handling practices.

As of this writing in the US most laws and ethics focus on data privacy. Healthcare and education have established laws. However, many legal and ethical issues involving the use of data are not worked out. Much work remains to be done in these areas.

Limitations

Finally, recognizing one's limitations is essential; acknowledging that data analysts aren't miracle workers and that inherent data flaws may pose constraints is crucial for managing expectations effectively. Despite efforts, sometimes there is no hope to salvage flawed data, leading to occasional dissatisfaction. Nevertheless, it's imperative to acknowledge and openly communicate one's limitations in analytical powers.

In summary, professional practices in data wrangling encompass project management, diligent documentation, adherence to ethics and laws, and recognizing limitations. Embracing these practices ensures effective and ethical data handling, fostering trust, collaboration, and reproducibility in the field of data analytics.

Example

Emma, a data analyst at a healthcare research firm, was assigned to clean and prepare a large dataset for a new study on patient outcomes. Following professional practices was critical for the project's success.

First, Emma applied project management skills by creating a detailed project timeline. She divided the work into phases—data acquisition, cleaning, validation, and reporting—and used a project management tool to track progress and assign tasks to team members.

Throughout the project, Emma emphasized documentation. She maintained a clear record of all data sources, listed every transformation applied to the datasets, documented the software used, and logged the dates each step was completed. This detailed documentation ensured that the project was transparent and reproducible.

Recognizing the importance of laws and ethics, Emma ensured all patient data was handled in compliance with HIPAA regulations. She anonymized the data before analysis and restricted access to only authorized personnel. She also consulted the legal team to ensure all practices met institutional standards for privacy and data protection.

Finally, Emma encountered significant gaps in the data—several patient records were missing critical outcome variables. Acknowledging her limitations, she reported these issues clearly to the research leadership, explaining how the missing data could affect the study's conclusions. Rather than trying to "fix" the flaws without proper information, she recommended cautious interpretation of the results.

By following professional practices in project management, documentation, ethical compliance, and recognizing limitations, Emma helped ensure that the data wrangling process was responsible, transparent, and trustworthy.

Data Source Issues

Comprehending the origin and sources of your data is fundamental in data analysis. While this may appear self-evident, it's frequently disregarded. Seldom will the data be exclusively yours; it may originate from diverse sources such as small enterprises, research endeavors, or public databases. Regardless, understanding its provenance is indispensable for responsible analysis.

Data collection techniques span a wide spectrum, from automated systems to manual entry, with each approach impacting the data's quality and the level of wrangling required. Typically, manually input data is more susceptible to errors, necessitating more extensive data wrangling. However, grasping the data collection method is pivotal for effective analysis.

Furthermore, it's crucial to ascertain whether the data is original or has been altered. For instance, healthcare claims data, while valuable, may not be the primary medical record and could have undergone modifications. Insight into the data's alterations and its original source is vital for precise analysis.

Additionally, verifying the legality of the data source is paramount. If it's your data or data from your business, it's likely legal to work with. Similarly, if you've obtained data with permission from a publication, contract project, or work project, it's probably legal to use. Most public data, including government data, is legal to use, regardless of whether it's posted on the internet or not. However, it's essential to verify the legality of the data source to avoid any potential issues.

GitHub mainly caters to computer science individuals rather than data professionals, so be cautious about using data from there. Kaggle, on the other hand, is a popular platform that vets its data. Scraping data off the internet comes with uncertainty surrounding laws and regulations.

If the data is questionable or its source is dubious, it's best to avoid using it.

Unfortunately, not everyone is honest, and there have been instances where high-profile scientists faced consequences for plagiarism. Avoid obtaining data from individuals with a history of fraud convictions.

When using data, knowing its origin is crucial. If the data has an untraceable source or is AI-generated, it may not be reliable for serious analysis due to potential legal complications. While AI-generated data may be suitable for student projects, it's not recommended for professional use.

Review Questions

1. What's the difference between coding and non-coding tools? When should each be used?
2. Why is documentation important in data wrangling? What should be documented?
3. What are the pros and cons of non-coding tools like Excel? When is coding needed?
4. How does project management help in data wrangling?
5. Why is knowing the data source and legality important? Provide examples.

1-3 Data Type and Form

Learning Outcomes

1-3-1 Understand how to import data from files or databases.

1-3-2 Recognize the difference between structured and unstructured data.

1-3-3 Cite examples of unstructured and structured data.

1-3-4 Understand how different file types affect data analysis.

1-3-5 Learn the importance of using the correct data type for accurate analysis.

Importing data involves bringing it from external sources or files to the analytical software being used. Data comes in different types and in different forms. In the past, this typically involved files on physical drives or CDs, but nowadays, data is often accessed online. Whether it's a standalone file or a database connection, skill in importing data is essential for analysis. Often, in a corporate setting, access to the SQL backend corporate data source via an internet connection is provided. Although you may lack computer science expertise to modify the data, you can still access it for analysis purposes, a common practice.

Structured vs Unstructured

Raw data refers to information directly from the source, such as original medical records rather than processed claims. Even processed claims are considered somewhat raw. Raw data can be categorized as structured or unstructured. In this book, we primarily focus on structured data due to the limited development of techniques for working with unstructured data.

Structured data typically comes in the form of easily importable row tables, often already processed to some extent. Most computerized systems, like medical records and sales data, tend to have structured data, though columns may contain text data for feedback, etc.

On the other hand, unstructured data includes text and image data. Semi-structured data lies in between, featuring XML markup tags, making it somewhat easier to handle than completely unstructured data. Although its definition may seem a bit ambiguous, semi-structured data lies between being fully unstructured and being organized in a table format.

File and Type

Overall, understanding file and data type is crucial for effective data manipulation and analysis.

File type refers to the specific format of the file, with some being proprietary and others nonproprietary. Nonproprietary file types, like CSV, are universal and can be read in various programs, whereas proprietary ones, such as Excel, are owned by specific entities.

For instance, SAS and SPSS formats, like .sav files, are heavily proprietary and may not be easily opened in other software. Converting file types is possible, but it's essential to exercise caution as the data's interpretation may change during the process. Proprietary file types, like PDFs, can pose challenges, particularly when attempting to extract data tables. Excel can aid in this process, but learning scanning techniques may be necessary. Handwritten data still exists, and even in statistics classes, some students prefer to conduct surveys by hand rather than using digital methods like Google Forms. This poses additional challenges for data collection and analysis.

Spreadsheet data files present their own set of challenges. People often use spreadsheets as notepads, mixing actual data with miscellaneous notes. When importing such data, it's essential to ensure that only relevant information is included. Moreover, older versions of Excel had limitations on the number of rows and columns they could handle, which could result in data loss during analysis. Similarly, Google Sheets had constraints on the number of variables.

Another important consideration is the data type assigned to each column in a structured data file. Software typically assigns data types automatically, but they may not always be accurate. For example, zip codes are often classified as numeric data when, in fact, they are textual information. Therefore, it's necessary to review and adjust the data types accordingly to ensure accurate analysis.

Textual information such as zip codes should be treated as text data, not numeric, despite appearing as numbers. Therefore, adjusting and refining data types is necessary to ensure accurate analysis. Computer science practices excel in this regard by formally assigning data types, unlike spreadsheet programs, which may lack precision in handling data types. While numeric and text are primary data types, each system may have its own unique data type specifications, leading to a lack of standardization and potential complexity.

In many programs, date formats are not data types but rather display formats. In Excel, dates are essentially represented as the number of days since a specific reference date. The way dates are displayed is merely a format, which can be customized without altering the underlying data. Similarly, in software like SAS or SPSS, data formatting is distinct from data types. Formatting code may be necessary to adjust the appearance of data, but it does not change the fundamental data type.

Review Questions

1. What is the difference between importing data from a file and connecting to a database?
2. Why is it important to know how to import data for analysis?
3. What is the difference between structured and unstructured data?
4. Why is it important to know the type of file you're working with when importing data?
5. What can happen if you don't set the correct data type for a column?

1-4 Data Profiling

Learning Outcomes

1-4-1 Explain what data profiling is and why it's important.

1-4-2 Understand the role of metadata (like data dictionaries) in data profiling.

1-4-3 Follow a four-step process for data profiling.

1-4-4 Identify categorical and numeric data and know how to profile each type.

1-4-5 Create frequency tables and cross-tabulations for categorical data.

1-4-6 Spot common issues in categorical data (e.g., spelling errors) and fix them.

1-4-7 Use histograms and box plots to explore numeric data.

1-4-8 Use basic statistics (like averages and spread) to understand numeric data.

1-4-9 Document issues found during profiling and plan how to fix them.

Data profiling involves the initial analysis and examination of data to grasp its structure, quality, and content before proceeding with further analysis. The goal is to gain insights into various aspects of the data, such as its variables, patterns, anomalies, and overall quality. Essentially, data profiling serves as the groundwork for data wrangling, as it's crucial to comprehend the data thoroughly before manipulating it.

Profiling should be documented, although there's no strict set of rules dictating exactly how it should be conducted. This process extends beyond traditional exploratory data analysis, which primarily focuses on fundamental statistics like distributions and modes. Profiling encompasses variable types and involves a more comprehensive assessment of the data.

Existing Documentation

Ideally, you'll have access to a data dictionary accompanying your dataset, which can greatly facilitate the profiling process. However, if such documentation is unavailable, you'll need to undertake this task yourself by meticulously examining the data and identifying its variables. In cases where you're dealing with backend data from systems like electronic medical records, reaching out to the software company that makes the can be beneficial. They can often provide valuable insights into the data's nature, origin, and structure.

Metadata, which refers to data about data, plays a crucial role in this process. A data dictionary serves as a form of metadata, providing essential information about the dataset's structure and content. While high-end software like SAS may automatically generate data dictionaries, not all tools offer this convenience. Therefore, you may need to rely on manual methods to create metadata for your dataset, ensuring clarity and understanding. In such cases, reaching out to the data source for clarification is advisable.

General Guide

As a general guideline for data profiling, consider this four-step process:

1. Review data source, content and structure.

2. Profile categorical variables.

3. Explore numeric data.

4. Document issues and plan to address.

Start by thoroughly reviewing the data source, examining its content and structure. Categorize and profile your variables, distinguishing between categorical and numeric types. While numeric variables allow for basic statistical analysis, such as means and medians, categorical variables require different techniques, like frequency distributions. Document any issues encountered during profiling and outline your plan to address them.

Review source, content and structure

When reviewing the data source, consider its reliability and timeliness. Outdated data may not be suitable for analysis, as the relevance of information often depends on its recency. Evaluate the dataset's content to ensure it includes the necessary variables for your analysis goals. Don't invest time cleaning data that lacks essential variables; instead, seek alternative data sources or adjust your analysis plan accordingly.

What is the content of the data? Are the variable names meaningful and reflective of the data they represent? Do you comprehend the data? Analyzing data without understanding it is futile. Ensure you have a reasonable grasp of the data's characteristics and nuances. While you may need to figure out some aspects as you go, you should have a basic understanding before starting the analysis. If you're uncertain about the data, consider conducting research or consulting with domain experts, including those involved in creating the software, collecting the data, or managing the project. It's essential to clarify any uncertainties early on to avoid wasting time.

Is the content of the data current or is there more recent data available if the current dataset is outdated? Exploring newer data sources can ensure the relevance and accuracy of your analysis. To obtain updated data, such as this year's sales data, if you were provided with sales data from last year, simply reach out to the source and request the current data.

What is the structure of your data? Is it aggregated or granular? Aggregated data, such as summarized figures like the number of students per major, may lack individual details but can be acceptable depending on the context. Is your data in a long or wide format? You may need to restructure it to align with your analysis goals.

Profile categorical data

When it comes to profiling categorical variables, categorical data, which is non-numeric, can be analyzed effectively using frequency tables. These tables can reveal various issues within the categorical data. Excel pivot tables can be a great way to make a frequency table of categorical data easily. Here are some basic examples generated for illustration purposes. Common issues like spelling errors can be easily corrected using Excel functions such as find and replace. Capitalization inconsistencies can also be resolved using Excel functions.

Product Name	Frequency
Smartphone	2
Laptop	2
Camera	1
Lapot	1
Camra	1
Smartfone	1

Another technique you can employ is cross-tabulation, which involves examining the relationship between two variables. In statistics, we often conduct chi-square analysis for this purpose. However, if you notice anomalies, such as all females receiving Fs and all males receiving As in a cross-tab, it indicates potential bias in your data. While you don't alter the data during analysis, such findings provide insights into data integrity.

	Grade		
Gender	A	B	C
Female	12	18	13
Male	14	21	22

Categorical variables can be graphically represented using various methods, such as frequency charts. While visually appealing, the primary goal of data profiling isn't aesthetics but rather diagnostic insights. Graphs serve as tools for data visualization and communication, aiding in understanding rather than beautifying the analysis process.

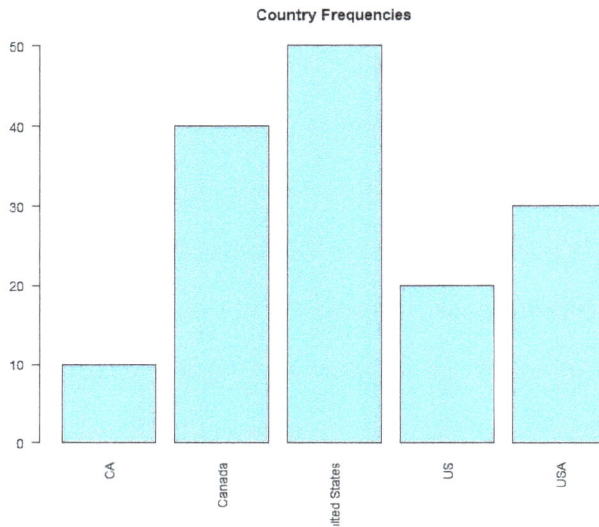

For instance, mosaic plots visualize relationships between two categorical variables, offering valuable insights for analysis.

Region vs. Satisfaction

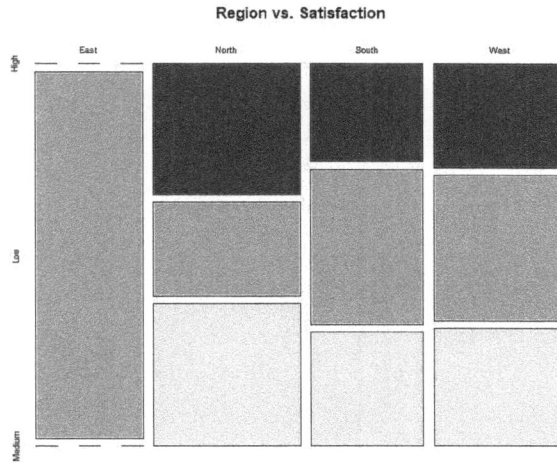

Explore numeric data

For numeric data, frequency tables remain a useful tool, although not applicable to all data types. Binning quantitative data, commonly taught in introductory statistics courses, allows for better understanding of data distributions.

Interval	Frequency
10 - 19	4
20 - 29	7
30 - 39	2
40 - 49	0
50 - 59	0
60 - 69	0
70 - 79	0
80 - 89	0
90 - 99	1

Histograms are another essential tool for visualizing data distributions, often covered in introductory statistics courses.

Histogram of Skewed Data

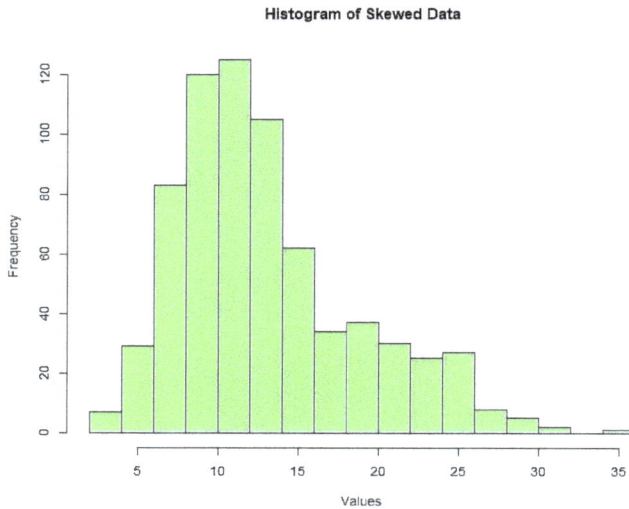

Box plots are valuable for identifying outliers and understanding data distribution characteristics.

Boxplot with Outliers

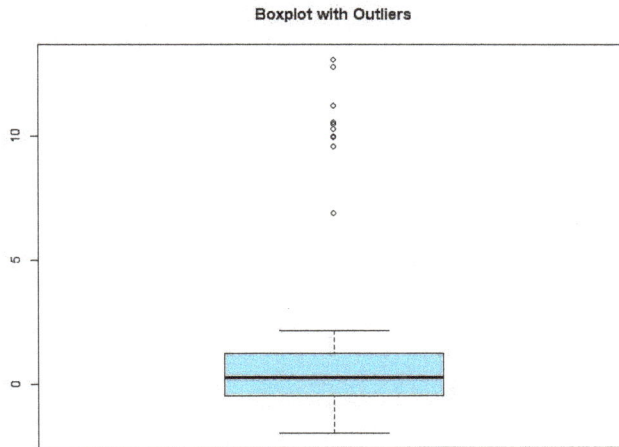

Summary metrics, such as measures of central tendency and measures of dispersion, provide additional insights into data characteristics. Utilize basic descriptive statistics tools, such as those available in Excel's Data Analysis Toolkit, to gain insights into your data.

Age	
Mean	40.28
Median	39.50
Mode	41.00
Standard Deviation	11.64
Range	46.00

When examining your quantitative data, it's essential to review basic revisit fundamental concepts, such as measures of center and measures of spread, typically covered in introductory statistics courses. These metrics provide valuable insights into the data's characteristics and data abnormalities and issues may be elucidated by reviewing them.

Documentation

Once you've completed the profiling process, document any issues you've identified. Keeping a record of these issues will guide you in addressing them effectively. Come up with a plan and timeline to address the issues.

Review Questions

1. What is data profiling, and why is it important?
2. How do data dictionaries help in data profiling?
3. What are the four steps in data profiling, and why is each important?
4. How can you tell the difference between categorical and numeric data?
5. What are some common problems in categorical data, and how can you fix them?
6. What is binning, and how does it help with numeric data?
7. How do histograms and box plots help you understand numeric data?
8. What do measures like averages and spread tell you about numeric data?
9. Why is it important to document the issues found during data profiling?
10. What challenges might you face if there is no data dictionary, and how can you overcome them?

Chapter 2

FOUNDATIONAL SKILLS

Some common foundational skills are often used in data analytics for wrangling tasks. Most of these can be done using spreadsheet software and are also implementable in most programming environments. Having spreadsheet skills is essential for various data-related tasks.

2-1 Sorting data

Learning Outcomes

2-1-1 Understand why sorting is useful in cleaning and organizing data.

2-1-2 Use sorting to find errors, outliers, and duplicates.

2-1-3 Know how to sort data correctly in Excel without breaking the dataset.

While it may appear trivial, sorting data plays a crucial role in data wrangling. It involves rearranging rows based on specific criteria such as alphabetical, numeric, or chronological order. Sorting facilitates the identification of outliers and inconsistencies in data sets. For instance, sorting data by time frames can help detect data entry errors, like a date recorded in 1920 instead of 2020.

The primary purpose of sorting is to organize data, making it easier to locate and identify patterns or issues within the dataset. Sorting can group data based on common attributes, making it convenient to analyze subsets of data. In Excel, sorting is a fundamental tool for data manipulation, allowing users to organize and analyze data efficiently. In the accompanying screenshot, you can see an example of data sorted in Excel where data cleaning issues can be identified.

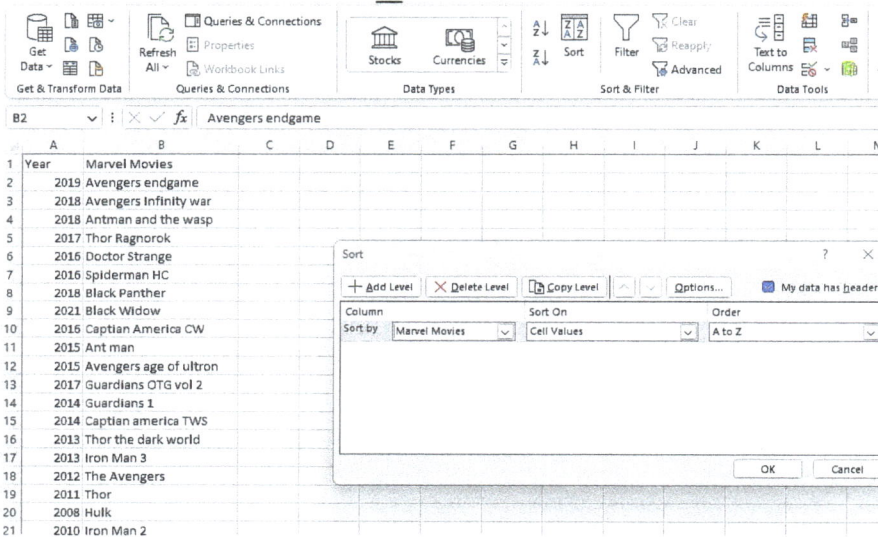

Sorting can be particularly useful with date sorting and outlier detection. By sorting data, you can quickly pinpoint discrepancies and anomalies. For instance, sorting data chronologically can highlight outliers or data entry errors, enabling timely corrections. Additionally, sorting aids in detecting duplicates, as repeated entries become conspicuous upon visual inspection.

D12	⌄	:	✕ ✓ ƒx	

◢	A	B	C	D
1	Year	Marvel Movies		
2	2015	Ant man		
3	2018	Antman and the wasp		
4	2015	Avengers age of ultron		
5	2019	Avengers endgame		
6	2018	Avengers Infinity war		
7	2018	Black Panther		
8	2021	Black Widow		
9	2011	Captian americ		
10	2016	Captian America CW		
11	2014	Captian america TWS		
12	2019	Captian Marvel		
13	2016	Doctor Strange		
14	2014	Guardians 1		
15	2017	Guardians OTG vol 2		
16	2008	Hulk		
17	2008	Iron man 1		
18	2010	Iron Man 2		
19	2013	Iron Man 3		
20	2002	spiderman 1		

Sorting also serves as a validation tool, especially for numerical data, ensuring that values fall within expected ranges. For instance, age data should typically range from 0 to 100 years, making values like -10 obvious outliers.

| N15 | ⌄ | ⋮ | ✕ ✓ | *fx* | |

	A	B	C	D	E
1	ID	Name	Age	Salary	Date Joined
2	3	Alice Brown	35	$60,000	3/20/2022
3	4	Bob Johnson	35	$55,000	4/25/2022
4	5	Carol White	40	$50,000	5/30/2022
5	6	David Black	45	$48,000	6/7/2022
6	7	Eve Green	30	$65,000	7/12/2022
7	8	Frank Lee	28	$58,000	8/15/2022
8	9	Grace Liu	35	$52,000	9/20/2022
9	13	Grace Liu	35	$52,000	9/20/2022
10	10	Harry Chen	32	$70,000	10/25/2022
11	11	Irene Wang	28	$55,000	11/30/2022
12	12	Jack Wu	38	$53,000	12/5/2022
13	2	Jane Smith	30	$45,000	2/15/2022
14	1	John Doe	25	$50,000	1/5/2022
15	14	Larry Tan	29	$45,000	2/15/2023

When sorting data in Excel, it's crucial to ensure that you're sorting the entire dataset and not just individual columns. While Excel permits sorting by specific columns independently, it's not advisable, as it can lead to confusion and errors as it dissociates the data.

Review Questions

1. Why is sorting helpful when cleaning data?
2. How can sorting by date help you spot errors?
3. What happens if you sort only one column in Excel?
4. How can sorting help you find duplicate or unusual values?

2-2 Filtering data

Learning Outcomes

2-2-1 Understand how filtering helps focus on specific parts of a dataset.

Filtering enables you to view a subset of data without permanently altering the dataset. By selectively displaying specific groups or categories, filtering helps focus your analysis on relevant information. In Excel, you can activate filtering by clicking on the filter icon and then applying filters to individual rows based on your criteria. This allows for the identification of patterns, trends, and outliers within the dataset.

2-3 Conditional formatting

Learning Outcomes

2-3-1 Use conditional formatting to highlight key data or errors.
2-3-2 Create simple formatting rules in Excel for numeric or text values.

Conditional formatting is another valuable tool often underutilized. It allows you to apply formatting to cells based on specific conditions or criteria. While conditional formatting can enhance the visual presentation of data, its primary purpose is to highlight important information or identify trends within the dataset.

To highlight errors or anomalies within your data, conditional formatting is an invaluable tool. With conditional formatting you can easily identify outliers and patterns that may require further examination. This feature is particularly helpful for spotting discrepancies or missing data points.

Conditional formatting in Excel is rule-based, allowing you to specify which

cells to format and how to format them. While it's most effective with numeric data, it can still be applied to text data as well. You have the flexibility
to choose the formatting style, such as highlighting cells in red, green, or yellow, depending on your preference.

To apply conditional formatting in Excel, navigate to the Home tab, click
on Conditional Formatting, and choose the desired format type. You can
customize the rules to suit your needs, such as formatting cells between
certain value ranges or based on specific criteria.

Here's an example of conditional formatting used to identify outliers in a
dataset. In a student survey about daily water consumption, cells containing
values outside the expected range are formatted in red. This makes it easy
to pinpoint entries that may require correction or further investigation.

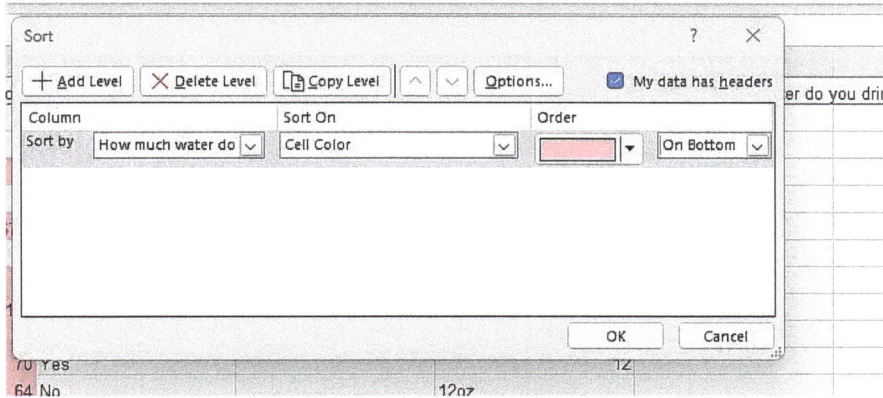

Once you've applied conditional formatting, you can sort the data based on the formatting criteria. This allows you to gather all erroneous entries in one place, making it easier to address them systematically.

Review Questions

1. What does conditional formatting help you do in a dataset?
2. How can it be used to spot data entry errors?

2-4 Pivot tables

Learning Outcomes

2-4-1 Summarize and analyze data using pivot tables.

2-4-2 Apply filters and sort data within pivot tables.

2-4-3 Identify data issues like misspellings using pivot tables.

The primary purpose of pivot tables is to provide a convenient way to summarize and aggregate data, which would otherwise be challenging to achieve manually. They offer dynamic functionality, meaning they adjust automatically as you modify the underlying data in your spreadsheet. While you may need to refresh the pivot table after making changes, it dynamically reflects those changes.

	Row Labels ⟲	Count of Name of Store
2		
3	Row Labels ⟲	Count of Name of Store
4	Amazon	2
5	Costco	1
6	Crystal Rock	3
7	Crystal Springs	1
8	Culligan Water	1
9	Distillata	4
10	ElDorado	1
11	Home Depot	1
12	LeBleu	1
13	Ready Refresh	2
14	Sparkletts	2
15	Walmart	1
16	Grand Total	20
17		

Pivot tables are often used for aggregating and summarizing data, particularly for generating frequency tables and percentages. However, they can also be used for other summary statistics like summing and averaging data, making them versatile tools for various analytical tasks. In business settings, pivot tables are commonly used for summarizing accounting data and other financial metrics.

One of the key features of pivot tables is their ability to filter and sort data, not only within the pivot table itself but also in conjunction with the original dataset. This becomes especially useful when dealing with large datasets where filtering and sorting can help navigate and analyze the data more efficiently.

Additionally, pivot tables allow you to slice and dice the data, enabling you to examine different subsets and dimensions of your dataset. Moreover, pivot tables serve as a foundation for creating charts and graphs to visually inspect data.

As a tool for data cleaning, pivot tables enable us to easily identify inconsistencies in the data, such as misspellings and categorical data errors. For instance, if you have a dataset with five color categories, and someone misspells "yellow" with one "L" instead of two, pivot tables can quickly flag such minor errors. Then Excel's Find and Replace feature is often sufficient to address these issues, rather than delving into programming languages like Python and having to write code to do simple data fixes.

Review Questions

1. What is the main purpose of a pivot table?
2. How do pivot tables help with data cleaning?
3. What types of summaries can pivot tables create?

2-5 Functions

Learning Outcomes

2-5-1 Students will use functions to clean and analyze data.

Excel boasts a vast array of built-in functions, covering everything from mathematical and statistical operations to financial calculations and text manipulation. While Excel's abundance of functions can sometimes be overwhelming, they provide powerful tools for data manipulation. For example, the text manipulation functions are particularly useful for cleaning data, as they can easily handle tasks like fixing capitalization errors without the need for complex coding.

In addition to mathematical and statistical functions, Excel also offers functions for working with dates and times. These functions are invaluable for tasks involving temporal data analysis and manipulation. Overall, mastering Excel functions is essential for efficient data cleaning and analysis.

Some functions Excel provides that are handy for data wrangling are in the table below.

Function	Description
VLOOKUP	Looks for a value in the leftmost column of a table and returns a value in the same row from a specified column.
HLOOKUP	Looks for a value in the top row of a table and returns a value in the same column from a specified row.
INDEX	Returns the value of a cell in a specified row and column of a table or range.
MATCH	Returns the relative position of an item in a range that matches a specified value.
IF	Checks whether a condition is met, and returns one value if true and another value if false.
SUMIF	Adds the cells specified by a given condition or criteria.
SUMIFS	Adds the cells in a range that meet multiple criteria.
COUNTIF	Counts the number of cells within a range that meet the given condition.
COUNTIFS	Counts the number of cells in a range that meet multiple criteria.
AVERAGEIF	Returns the average (arithmetic mean) of all cells that meet a given condition.
AVERAGEIFS	Returns the average (arithmetic mean) of all cells that meet multiple criteria.
CONCATENATE	Joins two or more text strings into one string.
LEFT	Returns the leftmost characters from a text string.

2-6 Graphical analytics

Learning Outcomes

2-6-1 Identify common graph types used in data wrangling.
2-6-2 Recognize the limits of graphical analysis in large datasets.

Spreadsheet programs such as Excel provide quick ways to make graphs of the data. While graphs can be helpful, especially for identifying outliers, it's essential to be mindful of their utility, particularly when dealing with large datasets. Graph creation can be distracting (and data visualization is another layer of the data analysis lifecycle after wrangling) and spending time creating visually appealing graphs can divert your focus from the primary objective which is to detect errors and anomalies.

Examples of graphs that are helpful in wrangling are line charts, scatterplots, histograms and boxplots. Line charts are great for looking at trends over time. Odd patterns in a line chart can identify problems in the data such as a missing chunk of data for a given time interval.

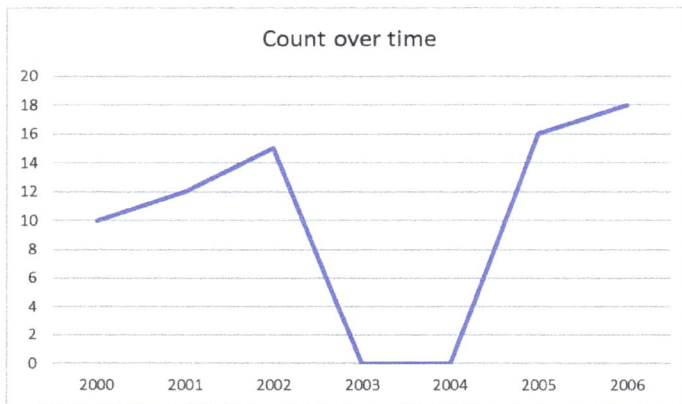

Scatterplots are the classic way to look at how two quantitative variables are related. For a relatively small data set scatter plots can be very useful. However, scatter plots may become overwhelming with even a moderate number of data points, hindering their effectiveness.

Histograms are visualizations of the frequency of the data and can be used to assess how the data is distributed. Distribution can take many forms such as uniform, normal or skewed. Although the histogram does not formally test for normality it can be helpful in determining if data needs adjustment to meet assumptions of normal distribution for further analysis. Histograms can also be helpful in detecting extreme outlier values.

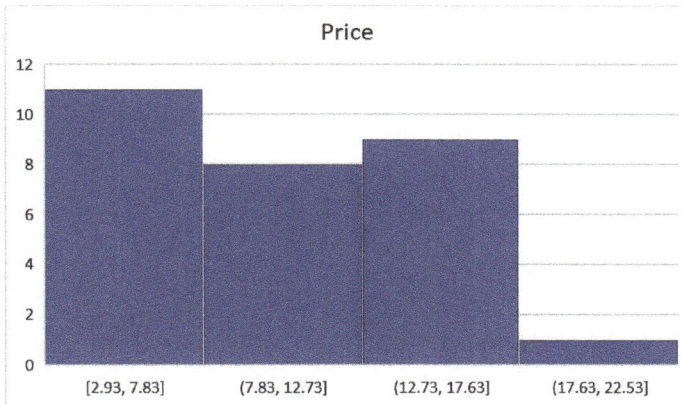

Price

Box plots serve a function like histograms in that they can be used to look at data distribution. Histograms are usually more practical due to their ability to display data distributions, while box plots excel at highlighting extreme outliers.

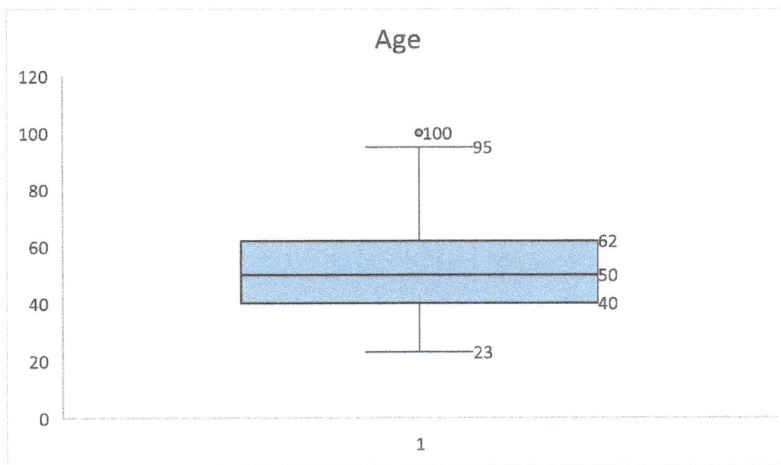

Age

It's crucial to understand the limitations of graphs, especially when dealing with large datasets. Many graphs used for presentation are not useful for assessing data quality, such as pie charts. Pie charts are primarily used for presentation and data communication, rather than assessing data quality. Many graphs are typically done on aggregated data which is not useful for examining raw data quality.

While graphs can be helpful, students should not rely excessively on graphical analysis for data cleaning and wrangling purposes. As datasets grow larger, graphical analysis becomes less useful, and alternative methods of assessing quality of data become more valuable.

Review Questions

1. Name two graphs useful for spotting outliers.
2. What kind of data is best shown with a line chart?
3. Why can scatterplots be less effective with large datasets?
4. How are histograms and boxplots different in their use for data wrangling?
5. Why are pie charts not helpful for assessing data quality?

2-7 Data Validation

Learning Outcomes

2-7-1 Explain why data validation matters for data quality.

Data validation is an important feature in Excel and other data input forms. Data validation ensures that data meets specific criteria before it is entered into the database. For instance, it verifies that when you input age, it is in numerical form. However, as a data analyst, you often lack control over this process, as it is typically handled by database programmers or others involved in data collection. Nevertheless, data validation is crucial during the design of any data collection system to ensure accuracy, consistency, and integrity by preventing incorrect data entry from the start.

Unfortunately, if data validation is overlooked during the design phase, data analysts may be left to deal with the consequences of inaccurate or inconsistent data. However, addressing these challenges can provide job security for data professionals.

In conclusion, proficiency in the foundational skills presented in this chapter is essential for effectiveness in data wrangling.

Chapter 3

DATA CLEANING

This chapter begins the official discussion of the data wrangling process itself with a focus on data cleaning. Recall the data wrangling process is a clear trajectory with the three-step process cleaning, modifying, and restructuring data.

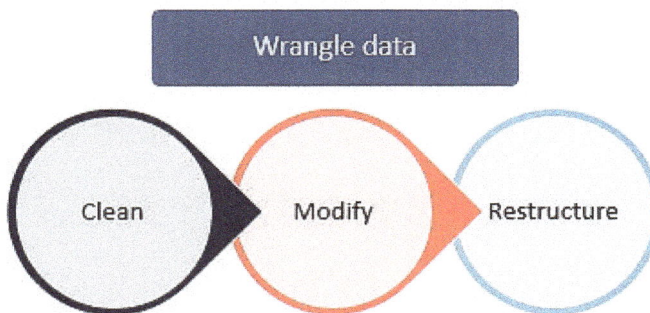

Data cleaning is the systematic process of rectifying issues within individual columns or variables. These issues could range from simple spelling errors to more complex formatting inconsistencies. It's crucial to retain the original, uncleaned dataset as a backup to mitigate any inadvertent changes during the cleaning process.

To guide our data cleaning efforts, let's follow the framework of "Pillars of Clean Data." These six characteristics—consistency, accuracy, validity, uniqueness, completion, and relevance—serve as benchmarks for assessing the cleanliness of our data.

Pillars of Clean Data

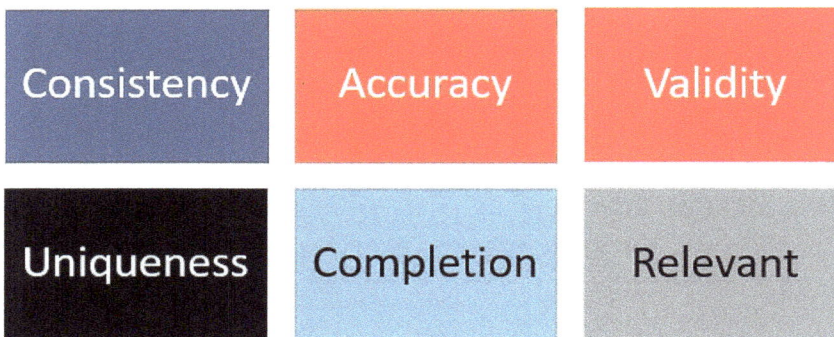

Consistency	Accuracy	Validity
Uniqueness	Completion	Relevant

3-1 Consistency

> **Learning Outcomes**
>
> **3-1-1** Explain what data consistency means and why it matters.
>
> **3-1-2** Spot examples of inconsistent data.
>
> **3-1-3** Use tools like frequency tables and Find and Replace to find and fix problems.
>
> **3-1-4** Fix text issues like spelling, capitalization, and different formats.
>
> **3-1-5** Standardize patterns in data like dates, phone numbers, and zip codes.
>
> **3-1-6** Use Excel functions like UPPER, LOWER, and PROPER to clean text.
>
> **3-1-7** Handle missing or unclear data carefully.
>
> **3-1-8** Adjust money values over time to make fair comparisons.

Data consistency implies uniformity and standardization. In clean data, similar data elements are represented in the same way across the dataset. Consistency is paramount in data integrity. Within a column, data should adhere to uniform standards. Text data, for example, should maintain consistent capitalization and spelling. Similarly, patterns such as phone numbers, zip codes, and dates should follow consistent formats. Units of measure should also remain consistent; mixing pounds and kilograms, for instance, introduces ambiguity.

Pillars of Clean Data

Data consistency implies uniformity and standardization. In clean data, similar data elements are represented in the same way across the dataset. Consistency is paramount in data integrity. Within a column, data should adhere to uniform standards. Text data, for example, should maintain consistent capitalization and spelling. Similarly, patterns such as phone numbers, zip codes, and dates should follow consistent formats. Units of measure should also remain consistent; mixing pounds and kilograms, for instance, introduces ambiguity.

Ensuring consistency begins ideally with data validation when the data is inputted. While an ideal system would prevent such inconsistencies, idealism is not the norm. Practical scenarios often require manual intervention, such as cleaning or omitting errant entries. Generally, the more humans enter the data is (vs automated) the less consistent the data is.

Inconsistent data presents challenges in interpretation. For example, if the field is an order date one would expect a calendar date to be entered. However, if manual entry is allowed a user may enter 'Friday' as the order date. This leads to issues with analyzing the data. In cases like this, resolving inconsistencies may require judgment calls, such as whether to amend the date with an order date (perhaps obtainable for another field) or to omit that data (making it missing data), though intentional data manipulation is never acceptable.

For example, consider data on consumption frequency where respondents input their responses freely. While the intended format is a number for specific days per week, entries like "every day" or "5 days" require conversion to a standardized format. However, discarding such data isn't always viable; data cleaning often involves striking a balance between salvaging usable data and discarding irreconcilable entries.

	A	B	C
1	**Frequency of Consumption**		
2	everyday		
3	everyday		
4	5 days		
5	everyday		
6	everyday		
7	2 days		
8	everyday		
9	4 days		
10	everyday		
11	everyday		
12	6 days		
13	everyday		
14	n/a		

Diagnosing consistency issues can be aided by generating frequency tables, especially in large datasets. This allows for a closer examination of response distributions, pinpointing areas of inconsistency.

	Row Labels ▼	Count of Frequency of Consumption
2		
3	Row Labels ▼	Count of Frequency of Consumption
4	1 day	14
5	2 days	15
6	3 days	15
7	4 days	18
8	5 days	18
9	6 days	10
10	everyday	46
11	n/a	21
12	(blank)	
13	**Grand Total**	**157**
14		

Tools like Excel's Find and Replace function can be invaluable for rectifying such issues, streamlining the cleaning process, even with complex datasets.

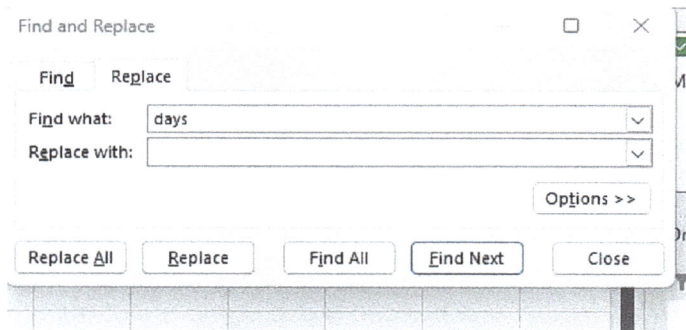

While it's tempting to jump into R or Python and start coding, the reality is that many data cleaning tasks can be addressed effectively in Excel. One common challenge is handling NA (Not Available) values. For instance, if a survey question asks about meat consumption per week and NA signifies non-meat eaters, you might consider replacing NA with a zero or leaving it blank. However, the interpretation of NA values depends on the context of the data and the analyst's discretion. Sometimes, creating a separate variable to indicate missing data or employing other strategies is necessary.

Consider another scenario with inconsistent numeric data, such as mixing numerical and textual entries in the age column. While this may seem straightforward to fix, it can be complex and difficult to do either in programming or a spreadsheet.

B	C	D	E	F	G
	name	age	email		
1	John		25	john@example.com	
2	Sarah		32	sarah@example.com	
3	Mark	forty		mark@example.com	
4	Lisa		28	lisa@example.com	
5	Michael	thirty		michael@example.com	
6	Emily		20	emily@example.com	
7	David		35	david@example.com	
8	Amy	twenty-nine		amy@example.com	
9	Robert		27	robert@example.com	
10	Jessica	thirty-one		jessica@example.com	
11	Brian		24	brian@example.com	
12	Amanda		33	amanda@example.com	
13	Joshua	thirty-two		joshua@example.com	
14	Natalie		22	natalie@example.com	
15	Patrick	forty-two		patrick@example.com	
16	Megan		26	megan@example.com	

Text data

Text fields pose unique challenges since they can accommodate any data type and text data is often hand entered (such as on fields for entry forms). Text inconsistencies are easily identifiable in frequency tables.

1		
2		
3	**Row Labels** ▾	**Count of Gender**
4	F	1
5	Female	5
6	M	2
7	Male	4
8	(blank)	
9	**Grand Total**	**12**
10		

Spelling, capitalization and different representations of the same data are common consistency problems (much of which data validation could have been prevented – for example by using drop down menus for common fields like salutation and gender.). Common inconsistencies in text data, like variations in gender representation (e.g., "Male," "Female," "M," "F"), can be addressed with Find and Replace or other text manipulation techniques.

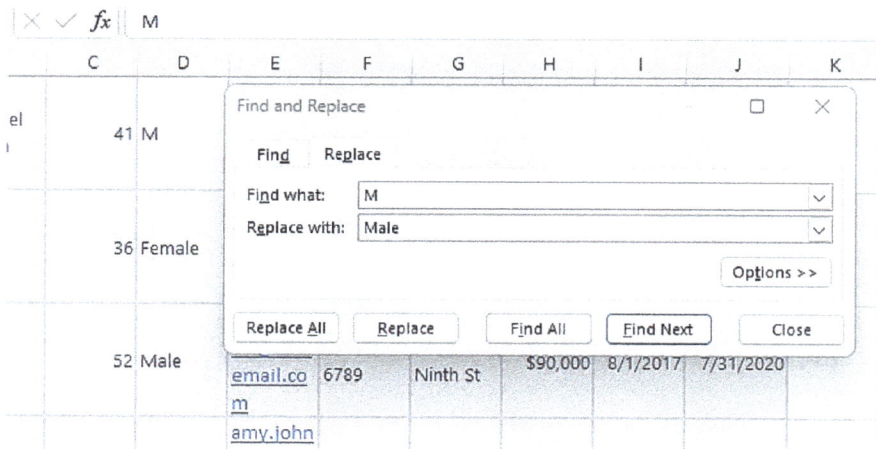

Beyond Find and Replace, Excel offers a plethora of functionality to aid in data cleaning. Spell check, for instance, is a valuable tool for addressing spelling errors, which are common entry mistakes.

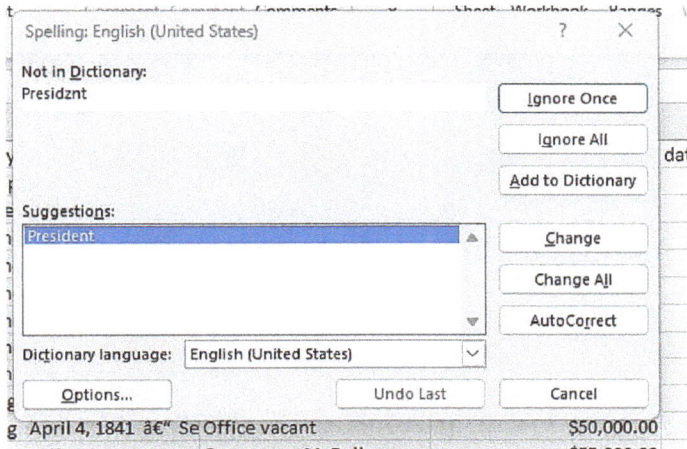

Similarly, case functions enable the standardization of text by converting to uppercase, lowercase, or proper case. For example, suppose you have messy data with inconsistent capitalization, like state abbreviations. Converting everything to uppercase using Excel's UPPER function is a quick fix.

Additionally, Excel provides LOWER which is a similar function to UPPER.

	A	B	C	D	E	F
		Clipboard ⌐		Font ⌐		Alignment
	E2	∨ : ✕ ✓ *fx*	=LOWER(A2)			
	A	B	C	D	E	F
1	Event		UPPER		lower	⌐
2	fRENCH reVOLuTIon		FRENCH REVOLUTION		french revolution	
3	amEriCAN reVOLUtion					
4	WOrLD wAr II					
5	EnLIGHTenment					
5	cIVIL rIGHTs moVEMENT					
7	gLobALIZATION					

The PROPER function acts by capitalizing the first letter of each word in a text entry.

	A	B	C	D	E	F	G	H	I	J
32		∨ : ✕ ✓ *fx*	=PROPER(A2)							
	A	B	C	D	E	F	G	H	I	J
	Event		UPPER		lower		Proper			
	fRENCH reVOLuTIon		FRENCH REVOLUTION		french revolution		French Revolution			
	amEriCAN reVOLUtion									
	WOrLD wAr II									
	EnLIGHTenment									

Patterns

Consistency of pattern is crucial for data integrity, especially with entries like dates, names, zip codes, and phone numbers. While allowing manual entry invites inconsistencies, tools like frequency tables can help identify patterns. Additionally, functions and even regular expressions can be employed to standardize formats, ensuring data consistency.

The example illustrated uses an Excel function that, while complex, serves a crucial role in data cleaning. This function essentially strips out non-numeric characters leaving behind only the numerical values. For instance, if Column A contains phone numbers in various formats, applying this function results in a clean set of numbers in Column C. From there, you can easily reformat the data to achieve consistency of the phone numbers.

	A	B	C
1			
2	PHONE NUMBER	FUNCTION	RESULT
3	(317) 873-5673	=(SUBSTITUTE(SUBSTITUTE(SUBSTITUTE(SUBSTITUTE(SUBSTITUTE(SUBSTITUTE(A3,"(","")",")","","),"-","",""),",",""),".","",""),"+",""))+0	3178735673
4	(+201). 456.7896		2014567896
5	312-765-8793		3127658793
6	208.658.9873		2086589873
7			
8			
9			

Date consistency

Dates pose a significant challenge in data consistency due to the myriad of formats they can take. Countries often have distinct conventions for data representation, including dates. For example, in Europe, dates are commonly written in the day-month-year format, while in the US, it's month-day-year. It's crucial to ensure consistency in date formats when analyzing data collected from different regions to avoid misinterpretation. In the example provided, dates are inconsistently formatted, with some in month-day-year and others in year-month-day formats. Standardizing these formats is essential for effective analysis.

ID	Name	Date	Amount
1	John Doe	1/15/2022	500.5
2	Jane Smitl	5/20/2023	750.25
3	Michael B	8/10/2021	1200.75
4	Sarah Johr	9/30/2022	900.8
5	David Wils	7/5/2023	600
6	Emily Dav	12/25/2022	1500.5
7	Robert Cla	11/8/2022	800.25
8	Amy Ande	2023/02/30	950.75
9	Thomas N	7/18/2022	1100.8
10	Jessica Le	4/25/2021	400
11	Mark Tayl	6/10/2022	1350.5
12	Amanda V	10/2/2022	700.25
13	Steven Ma	2021/09/40	1000.75
14	Laura Thoi	2/28/2022	950.8
15	Brian Harr	7/15/2023	650
16	Megan Ga	3/20/2022	1250.5
17	Christoph	6/12/2023	900.25
18	Kimberly I	5/18/2022	950.75
19	Matthew I	2022/09/35	1200.8
20	Stephanie	7/1/2023	550

Sorting is helpful to organize data so that dates to be fixed are together.

To address data inconsistencies, Excel's functionality and custom functions offer powerful tools for addressing them. Similar functions are provided in other programs and programming languages. It is important to make dates consistent before further analysis is performed using this data.

C	D	E	F	G	H	I	J	K	L	M	N	O
Name	Date	Amount		Date reformatted		=DATE(LEFT(A1,4),MID(A1,6,2),RIGHT(A1,2))						
8 Amy Ande	2023/02/30	950.75		2/30/2023								
19 Matthew	2022/09/35	1200.8		9/35/2022								
27 Daniel Le	2022/08/45	1000.75		8/45/2022								
13 Steven M	2021/09/40	1000.75		9/40/2021								
15 Brian Harr	2023-07-15	650										
5 David Wil	2023-07-05	600										
20 Stephanie	2023-07-01	550										

Units of measure

Another source of inconsistency is units of measure. Data on metrics like height and weight may be entered without specified units, leading to for example data on weight that can be in kilograms and pounds with no clarity as to what units are being used. If no units are provided further investigation is required to determine what units, the data are in and if it is consistent.

If the entries include units in the data, then addressing this is easier. Addressing this requires coding logic to standardize units, as demonstrated in an example dataset where weights are recorded in both kilograms and pounds. Logic in Excel with functions can be helpful to convert all units to a standard measure. Similar tasks can be accomplished in R or Python.

In the process illustrated below demonstrates use of a function to extract value of data. This is extracting the values in the data.

C15		f_x	=1/LOOKUP(2,1/--MID(A15,MIN(INDEX(FIND(ROW($1:$10)-1,A15&1/17),,)),ROW(INDIRECT("1:"&LEN	

	A	B	C	D
1	Weight		=1/LOOKUP(2,1/--MID(A2,MIN(INDEX(FIND(ROW($1:$10)-1,A2&1/17),,)),ROW(INDIRECT("1:"&LEN(A2)))))	
2	200 kg			200
3	12 lbs			12
4	3.5 kg			3.5
5	5.7 lbs			5.7
6	1.2 kg			1.2
7	8.2 lbs			8.2
8	15 lbs			15
9	18 kg			18
10	2.5 kg			2.5
11	0.4 lbs			0.4
12	5 kg			5
13	90 lbs			90
14	3.8 kg			3.8
15	28 lbs			28
16	0.6 kg			0.6
17	25 lbs			25
18	4.5 kg			4.5
19	0.8 lbs			0.8
20	1.2 kg			1.2
21	75 lbs			75

A logic function is used to determine if the data is in kg or not.

| E2 | | f_x | =ISNUMBER(SEARCH("kg",A2)) | | |

	A	B	C	D	E	F
1	Weight		value		is kg?	
2	200 kg		200		TRUE	
3	12 lbs		12		FALSE	
4	3.5 kg		3.5		TRUE	
5	5.7 lbs		5.7		FALSE	
6	1.2 kg		1.2		TRUE	
7	8.2 lbs		8.2		FALSE	
8	15 lbs		15		FALSE	
9	18 kg		18		TRUE	
10	2.5 kg		2.5		TRUE	
11	0.4 lbs		0.4		FALSE	
12	5 kg		5		TRUE	
13	90 lbs		90		FALSE	
14	3.8 kg		3.8		TRUE	
15	28 lbs		28		FALSE	
16	0.6 kg		0.6		TRUE	
17	25 lbs		25		FALSE	
18	4.5 kg		4.5		TRUE	
19	0.8 lbs		0.8		FALSE	
20	1.2 kg		1.2		TRUE	
21	75 lbs		75		FALSE	

A logic function and calculation are used to compute the weight in lbs. which makes the data consistent.

	G2		⌄	:	✕ ✓ $f\!x$		=IF(E2=TRUE,C2*2.2,C2)		

	A	B	C	D	E	F	G	H	I
	Weight		value		is kg?		weight in lb		
	200 kg		200		TRUE		440		
	12 lbs		12		FALSE		12		
	3.5 kg		3.5		TRUE		7.7		
	5.7 lbs		5.7		FALSE		5.7		
	1.2 kg		1.2		TRUE		2.64		
	8.2 lbs		8.2		FALSE		8.2		
	15 lbs		15		FALSE		15		
	18 kg		18		TRUE		39.6		
0	2.5 kg		2.5		TRUE		5.5		
1	0.4 lbs		0.4		FALSE		0.4		
2	5 kg		5		TRUE		11		
3	90 lbs		90		FALSE		90		
4	3.8 kg		3.8		TRUE		8.36		
5	28 lbs		28		FALSE		28		
6	0.6 kg		0.6		TRUE		1.32		
7	25 lbs		25		FALSE		25		
8	4.5 kg		4.5		TRUE		9.9		
9	0.8 lbs		0.8		FALSE		0.8		
0	1.2 kg		1.2		TRUE		2.64		
1	75 lbs		75		FALSE		75		

Similarly, the value of currency can vary over time, posing a challenge for longitudinal data analysis. It is not consistent to analyze data comparing values of money over time as historic price values are not comparable to current. Adjusting monetary values to maintain consistency across years often involves referencing tools like the US Government Consumer Price Index (CPI) to account for inflation. This ensures that comparisons between different time periods accurately reflect changes in purchasing power.

Review Questions

1. What does data consistency mean, and why is it critical for data analysis?
2. Give two examples of how inconsistency might appear in text data.
3. Why is manual data entry more prone to inconsistencies than automated data entry?
4. How can generating a frequency table help you spot consistency issues?
5. What Excel tool can you use to quickly replace inconsistent text entries?
6. Which Excel functions can help standardize text capitalization?
7. Why is maintaining a consistent pattern important for fields like phone numbers and dates?
8. What challenge can arise when dates are entered in different regional formats, and how can sorting help address it?
9. How would you handle a dataset where some weights are recorded in kilograms and others in pounds?

3-2 Accuracy and Validity

Learning Outcomes

3-2-1 Define accuracy and validity.

3-2-2 Identify outliers and describe their impact.

3-2-3 Use box plots, z-scores, and frequency tables to spot outliers.

3-2-4 Recognize data range issues and causes.

3-2-5 Explain set membership problems.

3-2-6 Detect cross-field validation errors.

3-2-7 Check computed fields for accuracy.

Pillars of Clean Data

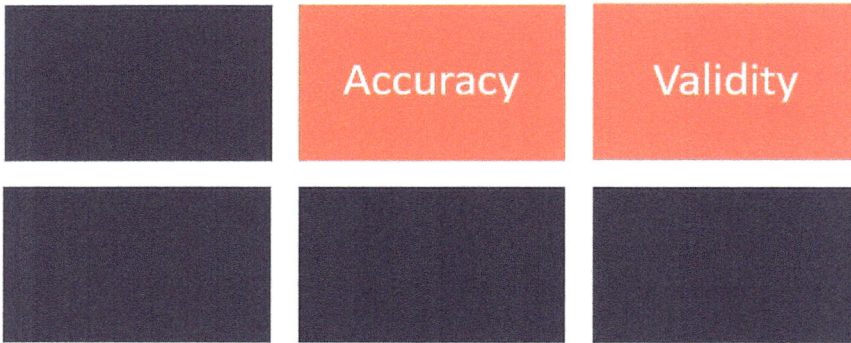

	Accuracy	Validity

Outliers are data points that lie significantly outside the range of other values in a dataset, impacting the accuracy and validity of our analysis. Accuracy ensures that data values are free from errors or mistakes, while validity refers to how well the data adheres to expected rules and constraints. For instance, representing someone's age as 120 instead of 12 would be an accuracy issue, while date stamps outside the expected timeframe would violate validity.

Accuracy and validity are closely related, as both contribute to the overall integrity of the data. Challenges related to accuracy and validity can manifest in various ways, including outliers, issues with set membership, and cross-validation.

Outliers can disrupt statistical analyses. Methods for identifying outliers are typically taught as part of a descriptive statistics unit in a statistics course and include using the 1.5 times IQR method and the method of using standard normal scores. Such methods you learn in basic statistics courses can be invaluable for identifying outliers. For instance, if you come across a score of -20 in your dataset, it's evident that this value doesn't make sense and would be considered both a validity and an outlier issue.

B	C	D	E	F
D	Name	Age	Score	
1	John Doe	25	75	
2	Jane Smitl	32	95	
3	Michael B	40	120	
4	Sarah Johı	27	85	
5	David Wil:	29	105	
6	Emily Dav	35	68	
7	Robert Clɛ	31	150	
8	Amy Ande	26	110	
9	Thomas M	42	-20	←
10	Jessica Leı	28	102	

Data range issues

When addressing accuracy and validity concerns, focus on identifying issues with the range of the data. Frequency tables are an excellent tool for understanding the distribution of data values and identifying any anomalies. Additionally, a box plot can be particularly useful for visualizing extreme values. In a box plot, outliers are represented as individual data points outside the range of the box.

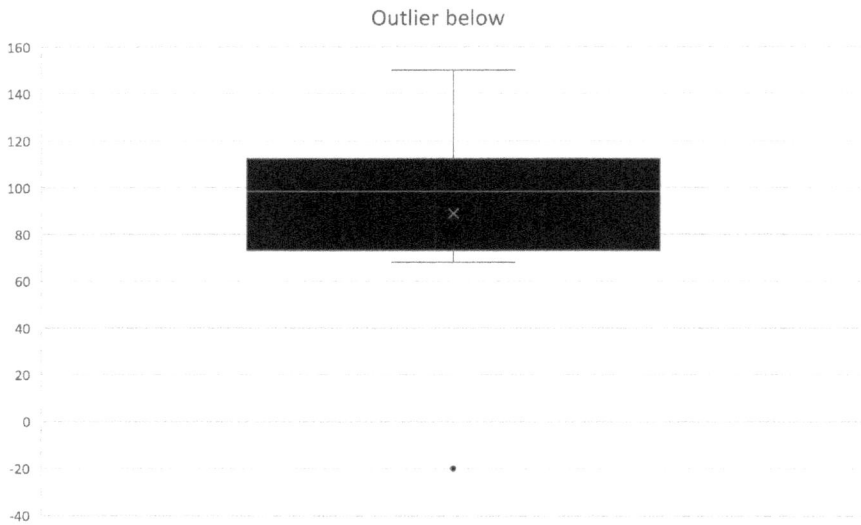

Outlier below

Basic statistical measures such as the minimum and maximum values provide insights into the data range. Moreover, metrics like the z-score, a measure of how many standard deviations a data point is from the mean, can help identify outliers. A z-score greater than two in either direction, or even more extreme values like plus or minus three, is typically considered indicative of an outlier. Recall, calculating z-scores requires standardizing the data by subtracting the mean and dividing it by the standard deviation.

Score	standard z score
75	-0.3120284
95	0.13372647
120	0.69092009
85	-0.089151
105	0.35660392
68	-0.4680426
150	1.35955244
110	0.46804264
-20	-2.4293642
102	0.28974068

Conditional formatting in tools like Excel offers a quick way to investigate potential data range issues. For example, you can highlight any score values between 1 and 100, as these are expected in most contexts.

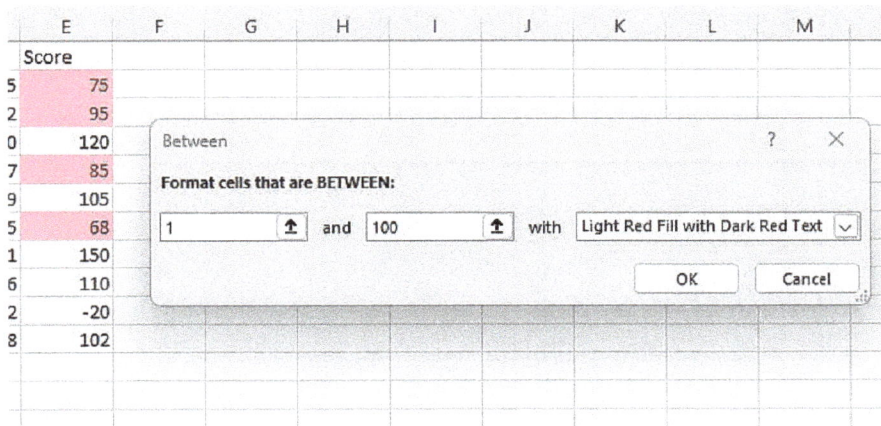

In cases where values between one and 100 are highlighted and others seem unusual, it's essential to investigate potential causes of data range issues. Are these values true outliers, representing exceptional performance? Sometimes, extreme values are valid data points, but they can also indicate errors or inconsistencies.

Data range issues can also be due to inconsistent units. For instance, mixing meters and centimeters can lead to disparities in numerical values with odd ranges when it is a unit not a range issue. Decimal issues, particularly prevalent in handwritten records, can also contribute to data range problems. For instance, a decimal point may be misinterpreted or omitted, resulting in erroneous data entries.

When addressing data range issues, the approach varies depending on the specific circumstances. Omitting problematic data points is an option but should be approached cautiously to avoid compromising the integrity of the analysis. It's essential to document any changes made and consider further investigation or consultation with relevant sources to verify the accuracy of the data.

Ideally, data validation measures, such as minimum and maximum restrictions, should be implemented during data entry to mitigate potential issues. However, in practice, such measures may not always be in place.

Set membership

Set membership pertains to categorical data, where values should align with predefined groups or categories. Ensuring coherence in groupings is crucial for accurate analysis and interpretation of categorical data. For instance, if a field is designated for colors, the data should only include color values, not unrelated entries like "toilet paper." This type of violation can be addressed by investigating and cleaning the data, possibly categorizing nonsensical entries under an "other" category while documenting the changes made.

Animal	N
Cat	34
Dog	32
Toilet paper	1

Cross field validation

Cross-field validation is another crucial consideration, focusing on the consistency between two or more related fields. For example, in fields like birth date and death date or start date and end date, there should be logical consistency. For instance, a death date should not precede a birth date, and an end date should not precede a start date. Detecting and rectifying inconsistencies in cross-field validation often involves calculating differences between dates and applying conditional formatting for validation.

Unlike one way frequency tables, cross-field validation may require additional calculations and comparisons between fields to identify inconsistencies. While crosstab tables can provide insights into relationships between categorical variables, table sizes can be challenging due to the potentially infinite combinations of variables.

An example of a cross-validation issue is when individuals have a death date preceding their birth date, an illogical scenario that requires investigation and correction. However, instances where individuals were born and died on the same day may represent stillborn births, which are plausible occurrences.

D	E
Name	Birth Date | Death Date
------------ --|------------|------------
John Doe | 05/15/1970 | 02/10/2022
Jane Smitl | 08/20/1985 | 04/05/1975
Alice Brov | 03/10/1990 |
Bob Johns | 06/25/1980 | 06/25/1980
Carol Whi | 12/05/1975 | 09/30/2023
David Blac | 02/14/1988 | 02/14/1988
Eve Green | 09/08/1972 | 09/08/2050

Another scenario where cross-validation issues may arise is in calculated columns, such as total weekly salary, derived from hourly wage multiplied by hours worked. Discrepancies between calculated values can indicate validity issues and necessitate reevaluation and potential recalculations.

Salary per Hour ($)	Hours Per Week (Hrs)	Total Salary per Week ($)	CHECK
16	32	450	512
0	0	0	0
15	10	85	150
15	32	446	480

Review Questions

1. What is the difference between accuracy and validity?
2. How do outliers affect data analysis?
3. How can a box plot help identify outliers?
4. What does a z-score tell you about a data point?
5. Name one cause of data range issues.
6. What is set membership?
7. Give an example of a cross-field validation issue.
8. How can conditional formatting help spot errors?
9. What should you do before removing an outlier?
10. Why is it important to check computed columns?

3-3 Uniqueness

Learning Outcomes

3-3-1 Explain why each record in a dataset should be unique.

3-3-2 List common reasons why duplicates happen.

3-3-3 Describe how bad joins can cause duplicate records.

3-3-4 Tell the difference between real duplicates and real repeated actions.

3-3-5 Use frequency tables and Excel to find and fix duplicates.

3-3-6 Understand why unique IDs are important.

3-3-7 Know how to safely remove duplicates without losing good data.

Pillars of Clean Data

In a clean dataset, each record should be unique to prevent analytical issues like double counting. Duplicates may arise from unintentional double entries or errors in data integration, such as in sloppy joins. Resolving duplicate records involves scrutiny and removal of redundant entries to maintain data integrity. Addressing duplicate records helps mitigate analytical problems stemming from double counting or overrepresentation of data points, ensuring accurate and reliable analysis outcomes.

The sloppy join issue occurs when one dataset has one record for an entity while the other dataset has two, potentially leading to accidental duplication of records. This issue underscores the complexity of joins, which, when mishandled, can result in significant data integrity problems. Naïve analysts may not notice these problems.

However, it's worth noting that not all duplicate records are unintentional. For instance, individuals may legitimately make multiple purchases of the same item on the same day. While these instances should ideally be accounted for with timestamps, they highlight the need to consider the context of the data before deeming records as true duplicates. Having a record of a person with the same name and birthdate and place of birth likely represents a genuine duplicate. In contrast, instances such as the same customer purchasing 22 items for $180 twice in one day may be more ambiguous and require closer examination to determine whether they are genuine duplicates or separate transactions.

Identifying duplicate records can be facilitated using frequency tables. For instance, a frequency table may reveal duplicate entries for a particular individual, prompting further investigation into their validity and potential removal to maintain data integrity.

	A	B	C	D
1				
2				
3	Row Labels ▼	Count of Name		
4	Alice Brown	1		
5	Bob Johnson	1		
6	Carol White	1		
7	David Black	1		
8	Eve Green	1		
9	Frank Lee	1		
10	Grace Liu	2		
11	Harry Chen	1		
12	Irene Wang	1		
13	Jack Wu	1		
14	Jane Smith	1		
15	John Doe	1		
16	Larry Tan	1		

Regarding the identification of duplicates, it's essential to exercise caution, even when individuals share the same name. Despite the assumption that no two individuals have the same name, common names and surnames can lead to multiple individuals sharing identical names. Personal anecdotes illustrate this point, as even the author has encountered numerous individuals with identical names and ages online, underscoring the need for thorough investigation before determining a record as a true duplicate.

Handling duplicate records can be facilitated through tools like Excel's "Remove Duplicates" feature or specialized database functions like the "No Duplicates" constraint. However, it's imperative to proceed with care, ensuring that duplicate removal is based on comprehensive criteria and not arbitrary selection. Selecting all relevant columns ensures a comprehensive assessment of duplicate entries, safeguarding against unintended data loss.

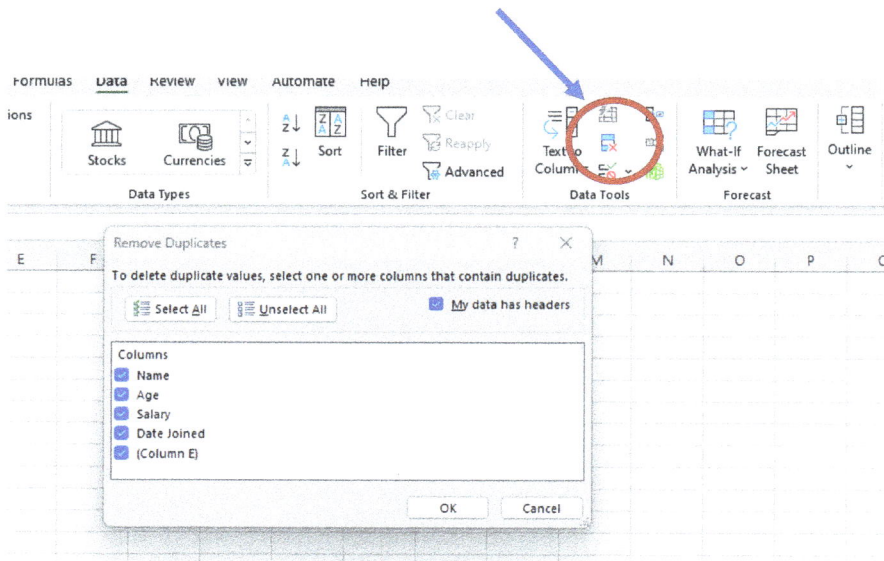

In an ideal backend database setup, unique identifier keys, such as student IDs, should guarantee record uniqueness. However, instances of duplicate identifier keys may occur due to data entry errors or system limitations. Such occurrences may necessitate collaboration with database administrators to rectify and maintain data integrity, especially if duplicates pose challenges for data merging or analysis.

Review Questions

1. Why should every record in a dataset be unique?
2. Name two reasons why duplicates might happen.
3. What is a sloppy join?
4. Give an example where two records look the same but are both correct.
5. How can a frequency table help find duplicates?
6. Why should you be careful when deleting duplicates?
7. What tool in Excel can help remove duplicates?
8. What is a unique ID, and why is it important?
9. Why should you select all columns when removing duplicates in Excel?
10. Who might you need to work with if you find duplicate IDs in a database?

3-4 Completion

Learning Outcomes

3-4-1 Explain the difference between missing and incomplete data.

3-4-2 Describe common methods for detecting and handling missing data.

3-4-3 Understand the risks and benefits of imputing missing values.

3-4-4 Recognize strategies to complete incomplete data using reference or inferred values.

Pillars of Clean Data

The issue of data completeness encompasses both missing and incomplete data. Handling missing or incomplete data requires the application of suitable techniques to ensure data integrity and accuracy. While missing data refers to the absence of information in a dataset, incomplete data signifies that certain observations or values are not fully recorded.

Missing data

Missing data can arise due to various reasons, including data entry errors, non-responses in surveys, equipment malfunctions, or simply because certain information was not collected. There are different types of missing data patterns. Missingness can occur randomly, but it can also be non-random, stemming from specific circumstances like system failures or intentional deletion. Detecting missing data can involve examining summary statistics, frequency tables, or using programming functions like `is.null` in R. Not every function or package can detect missing data, so it's important to exercise caution when detecting missing data and not overlook its existence. For instance, using a pivot table for frequency analysis may not always reveal missing values.

	A
1	Number
2	1
3	2
4	3
5	4
6	
7	1
8	1
9	2
10	2
11	3

2		
3	**Row Labels**	**Count of Number**
4	1	3
5	2	3
6	3	2
7	4	1
8	**Grand Total**	**9**
9		
10		

A significant challenge with missing data arises when calculating aggregate statistics. For example, if you calculate the average age based on available data but omit the missing ages, the accuracy of the result is uncertain. This is a serious analytical issue.

A	B	C	D	E	F
Student	Age				
1	12		Average	11.5	
2	11				
3					
4	12				
5	11				

Moreover, missing data can manifest at both the individual value field level and the entire row level. Ensuring the completeness of data requires verifying that all expected records are present. For example, in a dataset representing a class of 30 students, there should be exactly 30 rows of data.

Handling missing data

Handling missing data in analysis involves various strategies. Historically, filler values were sometimes used, but they often led to confusion and misinterpretation during data analysis. Common filler values included zeros, "N/A," "NaN," or other placeholder characters. It's important to note that filling missing data with zeros isn't usually advisable, except in specific contexts where it's meaningful, as demonstrated in an earlier example on the frequency of meat consumption per week. In this case if a person noted they do not eat meat imputing a 0 for a missing value in number of times meat is consumed per week is sensible.

One approach is to omit the missing values or rows entirely from the analysis, especially if they occur randomly and don't significantly affect the analysis such as when the data is missing at random and is a very small percentage of the data missing. However, if the missingness follows a non-random pattern, careful consideration is necessary to prevent biased analysis.

Imputation, which involves filling in missing data with educated guesses rather than random filler values, is a common practice. Imputing missing values should be done judiciously to avoid biasing the analysis. For example, if you have a city and ZIP code, you can infer the state. Similarly, if a student is in grade nine, you can estimate their age to be around 14 or 15. It's important to note when values have been imputed to maintain transparency in the analysis.

Alternatively, there are statistical methods, such as regression techniques, that can estimate missing values by leveraging a model to predict them. While we won't delve into these methods here, they involve using statistical principles to approximate missing values based on available data.

To handle missing data effectively, it's crucial to consider the context and explore various approaches. Seeking input from subject matter experts or individuals familiar with the data source can provide valuable insights. Mathematically, missing data can be addressed through techniques like imputation, where missing values are estimated based on existing data, but this requires a careful approach.

Incomplete data

Incomplete data, on the other hand, refers to data that lacks certain attributes or details, making it insufficient for analysis. Techniques for handling incomplete data may involve data imputation, where missing values are estimated or inferred based on existing data. For instance, you may have to match cities and states to ZIP codes in a reference table to complete the information. While this process may require time and effort, it's often necessary to ensure the usability of the data.

In summary, incomplete and missing data are typically treated similarly, and addressing them involves various strategies to maintain the integrity of the dataset.

Review Questions

1. What is the difference between missing data and incomplete data?
2. What is one strategy you can use to handle missing data in a dataset?

3-5 Relevant

Learning Outcomes

3-5-1 Define the concept of relevance in the context of clean data.
3-5-2 Identify examples of irrelevant data.

Pillars of Clean Data

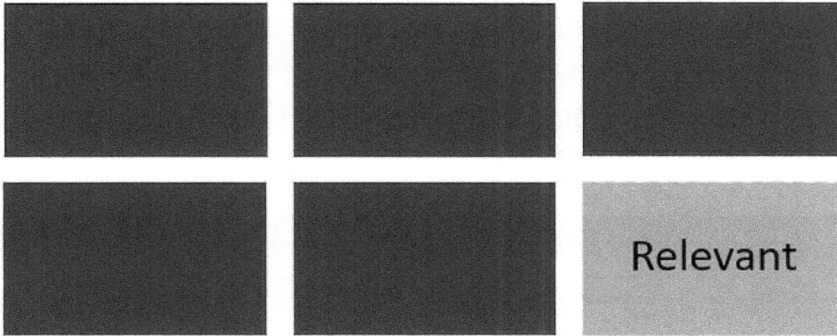

The final pillar of clean data pertains to the usefulness of the information included in the dataset. Unnecessary or irrelevant data should be avoided to ensure the dataset remains focused and efficient. Irrelevant data is simply not worth your attention. Additionally, the timeliness of the data is crucial.

Outdated information may no longer be relevant or accurate, highlighting the importance of regularly updating and maintaining datasets to ensure their relevance over time. Stale, outdated data usually falls into this category, as it's often not suitable for meaningful analysis. Whenever possible, opt for fresher data to ensure its relevance.

Other forms of irrelevant data include filler values, erroneous entries, and fields with no meaningful information. This mishmash of irrelevant content can be collectively referred to as "crud." Crud encompasses various issues like spacing inconsistencies, stray characters, random typos, and nonsensical entries that clutter the dataset. Fortunately, cleaning up crud isn't always a Herculean task. Excel offers helpful functions like "TRIM," which swiftly removes excess spaces from data fields.

Additionally, when cleaning data, consider whether certain fields are even necessary for your analysis. While it's wise to preserve them in the original dataset, you may choose not to include them in your analytical files to streamline your workflow. A common tactic in analysis is to extract only the essential fields for analysis, leaving extraneous data in the original dataset for reference but excluding it from further analysis. This approach of using a more computationally efficient smaller dataset for analysis helps maintain focus and clarity in the analysis process.

Review Questions

1. What does "relevance" mean in the context of clean data?
2. Why is it important to regularly update and maintain datasets?
3. Give three examples of irrelevant data that could appear in a dataset.

3-6 Signs of bad data

An overarching issue with clean data is the issue of a dataset which is just bad overall and should not be used in analysis for actionable results. Several issues flag such data.

A big flag in bad data is a suspicious amount of missing data. For instance, if there's a missing year in a dataset spanning 10 years, it raises questions about the data's integrity. Similarly, filler values like a series of 999s can be problematic and render the data unreliable. Incomplete data that only covers certain seasons or time periods may also pose challenges for analysis. For example, if sales data is available only for the months leading up to Christmas but not for the subsequent months, it limits the ability to analyze long-term trends accurately.

Moreover, excessive duplicates in the dataset, possibly resulting from errors in data joins, can hinder analysis and should be addressed before proceeding with any meaningful analysis. When you perform data joins, it's possible to inadvertently generate duplicates. While some duplicates can be resolved, an excessive number can lead to issues such as double or triple counting, creating confusion and inaccuracies in the dataset.

Another concern is the limitation of data storage capacity in older systems, which resulted in datasets that were truncated. Although this may not be as prevalent with modern technology, older systems, such as early versions of Apple spreadsheets, had limits on the number of columns and rows they could accommodate. For instance, with a column limit of 255, half of the data in a 500-column dataset would be lost. Similarly, Excel used to have a row limit of 65,536, which could truncate larger datasets. Consequently, data from older systems might be incomplete or cut off, potentially leading to discrepancies in data continuity. This truncation could explain inconsistencies, such as having only three months of data instead of six, particularly in older datasets. While modern software has likely addressed these limitations, it's essential to verify data integrity, especially when working with legacy datasets.

Furthermore, gross inconsistencies in the data can also signal problems. For example, if an aggregated dataset reports a sample size of 500, but the unaggregated dataset shows 750 entries, it raises questions about the missing 250 entries. Such discrepancies between different versions of the same dataset warrant investigation to ensure data accuracy and reliability.

Another indication of problematic data is when it deviates significantly from established norms or standards. For instance, if a random sample exhibits an 80% male composition while the population typically reflects a 50% male distribution, it raises concerns about potential biases based on factors like race, age, or gender. Biased data, often stemming from non-random sampling methods, represents one of the most significant and pervasive challenges in data analytics, yet it remains largely unaddressed.

Moreover, edited data poses another red flag. While some data cleaning and manipulation may be necessary, extensive editing or manipulation should be scrutinized, especially if the dataset is meant to remain raw and unaltered. Any alterations made should be documented in a log to maintain transparency and integrity.

Conversely, overly perfect data can also indicate potential issues. For instance, data with excessive precision, such as recording someone's weight to the ninth decimal place, is highly unusual and raises doubts about its authenticity. Similarly, data lacking natural variability, like consistently increasing values without fluctuations, is suspect since all natural data exhibits some degree of variability. Unrealistically precise or flawless data, such as knowing the exact number of stardust particles in Mars' atmosphere, should be approached with skepticism, as it may indicate errors or manipulation.

The ethical considerations surrounding data are complex and still evolving. Anything that violates research protocols, privacy laws, or ethical principles should raise red flags. For instance, if you come across medical data that appears to have been obtained unlawfully or lacks proper de-identification of patient information, it's essential to proceed with caution and question its origin.

Chapter 4

DATA MODIFYING

Recall this book is following the paradigm of cleaning data, modifying data, and restructuring data to provide a logical framework for data wrangling. Data modifying is the middle step of this process taking clean data and making any data level changes to it before any restructuring of the data takes place.

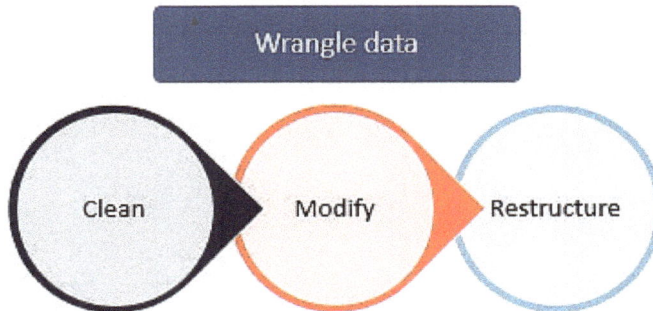

Data modification involves altering or changing existing data within specific fields of a database. It assumes that the data is already clean and is operated on to fulfill analytical purposes, such as normalization, standardization, or adjusting units. It's crucial to emphasize that data should be cleaned before modification. Ensuring data consistency and accuracy is paramount before embarking on any modifications. Use cases for data modification include changing variable names, adjusting units, reformatting data, joining or splitting fields, mathematically correcting skewed data, and binning or regrouping data.

Remember to always save your data before making modifications. It's advisable to save your progress step by step, especially when using tools like Excel. This practice ensures that you can backtrack if needed and minimizes the risk of losing valuable data.

Lastly, it's important to modify your data before restructuring it. There's no sense in restructuring data that hasn't been adequately modified and prepared for analysis. By following these principles, you'll ensure a smooth and effective data wrangling process.

4-1 Reassigning data types

Learning Outcomes

4-1-1 Recognize the importance of correct data types for analysis.

4-1-2 Identify common problems with data types (e.g., ZIP codes, units) and how to fix them.

4-1-3 Change data types in software like Excel and R.

4-1-4 Understand the difference between data types and formatting.

In this book, we take a software-agnostic approach, so we won't delve into specific programs and their respective data types. Excel, for instance, has a flexible approach to data types, while other software like SPSS, SAS, and R offer more predefined data types.

When we talk about data types, it's essential to understand that each column in analytics software is typically assigned a data type, either by the user or the software during data import. For example, in R with the Tidy verse, you can specify data types during data import. In Excel, you have some flexibility but may need to adjust data types manually.

Sometimes, you might need to change a data type, especially if it's automatically assigned and not suitable for your analysis. A common example is ZIP codes, which are often mistakenly interpreted as numeric data by software. However, ZIP codes should be treated as categorical data, not numeric. Assigning them as numeric data can lead to issues, such as leading zeros being dropped, resulting in incorrect ZIP codes. Therefore, it's crucial to review and potentially adjust data types to ensure accurate analysis.

If you mistakenly assign a ZIP code as a numeric field, it may be interpreted as a four-digit code, leading to significant errors if the leading 0 is dropped (and it often will be). Therefore, it's crucial to ensure that ZIP codes are correctly assigned as text fields, not numeric ones. This may require adjusting settings in some software to ensure accurate data handling.

Another common issue is including units in data entries, such as entering "30 pounds" in a weight column. However, this practice should be avoided as it converts the column into a text field rather than a numeric one. To maintain consistency, it's best to strip out the units from the data entries. While it's helpful to initially include units for clarity, they should be removed to maintain data integrity. Ideally, the units should be specified in the variable name, such as "Weight in kilograms," rather than within the data entries themselves.

These scenarios highlight the need to reassign data types to ensure accurate analysis. While the specifics of data type handling vary between software like Excel and R, creating a new variable and transferring the data while preserving the original column can be a practical approach.

Categorical encoding involves converting variables like gender into binary fields, which is commonly used in data mining and machine learning applications for simplicity. This transformation doesn't alter the data type but adjusts the representation for computational ease.

Data types should not be confused with formats. Formatting, on the other hand, doesn't change the data type; it simply modifies how the data is displayed. Unlike data type changes, formatting adjustments in software like SAS or Excel don't fundamentally alter the underlying data structure.

Review Questions

1. Why is it important to set the correct data type for each column in your data?
2. What happens if you treat ZIP codes as numeric data?
3. Why should you remove units like "pounds" from data entries?
4. How can you change a data type in Excel or R?
5. What is the difference between data types and formatting?

4-2 Date and time data

Learning Outcomes

4-2-1 Understand why date and time data can be tricky to work with.

4-2-2 Clean and standardize date and time formats for better analysis.

4-2-3 Format, modify, and calculate with dates in Excel.

4-2-4 Extract parts of a date, like month or year, for summaries and graphs.

4-2-5 Convert text entries into real dates.

4-2-6 Recognize that Excel stores dates as numbers behind the scenes.

4-2-7 Understand why it's important to account for different time zones.

Tackling date and time data can be a significant challenge for data analysts. These fields contain a wealth of information, including year, month, day, time, and sometimes time zone details. Moreover, date and time entries can vary in format and may contain incomplete or truncated information, making them complex to handle. If you encounter date and time data with multiple structures in a single field, such as start time, end time, and follow-up time, it's essential to standardize their formats for consistency (part of data cleaning). In some cases, users may input data manually, leading to inconsistencies that need to be addressed during the cleaning process. Ensuring uniformity in date and time formats is crucial for accurate analysis and interpretation.

However, once you've achieved consistency, it's time to consider modifications. For date and time data, these modifications might involve formatting adjustments, calculating date differences, adding or subtracting days, or extracting specific components like month or year. Converting text entries into recognizable date formats is another common task, especially when users input date data as text. Additionally, custom modifications may be necessary based on specific analytical needs.

Formatting dates

In Excel, dates are internally represented as the number of days since January 1st of a certain year, with various formatting options available for display. While Excel offers numerous date formats for presentation, remember that formatting changes only affect how data is displayed, not its underlying structure.

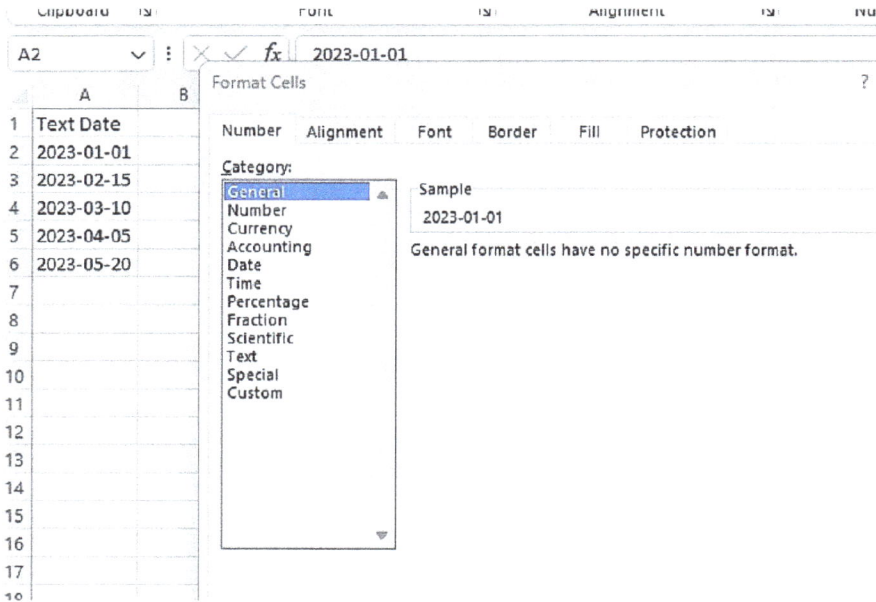

Computing differences between dates

When modifying data, you can also compute differences between dates, a task Excel simplifies through straightforward subtraction operations. For instance, calculating the duration between an end date and a start date is typically a straightforward process in Excel, provided the dates are correctly formatted and consistent.

Get & Transform Data | Queries & Connections |

C2	⌄ : ✕ ✓ *fx*	=B2-A2		
	A	B	C	D
1	**Start Date**	**End Date**	Days worked	
2	1/1/2023	1/10/2023	9	
3	2/15/2023	2/28/2023	13	
4	3/10/2023	3/20/2023	10	
5	4/5/2023	4/15/2023	10	
6				

Adding or subtracting dates

Moreover, adjusting dates by adding or subtracting days is often necessary for tasks like shifting start dates or including buffer periods. In Excel, such adjustments can be easily performed using arithmetic operations, allowing for efficient date manipulation within your dataset.

Get & Transform Data | Queries & Connections |

A2	⌄ : ✕ ✓ *fx*	=B2-3	
	A	B	C
1	Adjusted Start Date	**Start Date**	**End Date**
2	12/29/2022	1/1/2023	1/10/2023
3	2/12/2023	2/15/2023	2/28/2023
4	3/7/2023	3/10/2023	3/20/2023
5	4/2/2023	4/5/2023	4/15/2023
6			
7			

Extract date parts

You can also extract specific parts of a date, which is particularly useful for analyzing data over time and for creating time series graphs. Typically, displaying a time series graph for every single day of the year can make the visualization cluttered and overwhelming. Instead, it's common to plot weekly or monthly. To achieve this, you extract the relevant parts of the date, such as months or possibly months and weeks, and then average the data within those intervals to create a smoother time series graph.

Converting text to dates

Converting text entries into dates is another task you might encounter. Sometimes, date data is classified as text rather than actual date values. In Excel, you can use functions like DATEVALUE to convert text representations of dates into actual date values. Excel internally represents dates as the number of days since January 1st, 1900, although there might be minor inaccuracies due to leap year calculations. Nonetheless, for most purposes, this representation suffices.

Clipboard	⌐		Font		⌐		Alignm

B2   ∨   ⋮   ✕ ✓ *fx*   =DATEVALUE(A2)

	A	B	C	D	E
1	Text Date	Date Data			
2	2023-01-01	44927		Days since 1/1/1900	
3	2023-02-15	44972			
4	2023-03-10	44995		365.25*123	
5	2023-04-05	45021			
6	2023-05-20	45066			
7					

You can easily apply a date format to the values in a cell, such as B2, in Excel. Excel recognizes the date format based on the value, usually by the number associated with it. Once you've identified the date values, you can format them using Excel's date functions as per your preference.

Different time zones

Another crucial consideration when working with date and time data is accounting for different time zones. Nowadays, with people working remotely across various locations, it's essential to ensure consistency in time zones. For instance, when calculating hours worked, the time zone difference between employees in different locations needs to be addressed. Failing to do so may lead to inaccurate calculations. To address this issue in Excel, you can adjust the time frames accordingly. While in the past, when everyone was in the same physical location, time zone discrepancies were less of a concern. Nowadays, it's crucial to factor in different time zones when analyzing time-related data.

Review Questions

1. Why can date and time data be hard to work with?
2. Why do we need to standardize date and time formats?
3. Does changing the date format in Excel change the actual value?
4. How do you find the number of days between two dates in Excel?
5. When might you need to add or subtract days from a date?
6. Why would you want to pull out just the month or year from a date?
7. What Excel function helps you turn text into a real date?
8. How does Excel actually store dates?
9. What happens if you forget about time zones when working with time data?
10. Why are time zones more important today than in the past?

4-3 Normalizing and transforming

Learning Outcomes

4-3-1 Explain why normalizing data (using z-scores) is important.
4-3-2 Explain what a data transformation is.

Normalize and transforming are commonly done to convert data to different units before analysis. Normalization involves rescaling data for analytical purposes. By converting data into standard normal scores, we eliminate the influence of original units like inches or centimeters. This concept is often introduced in introductory statistics courses when discussing the normal distribution and z-scores. In many analytical contexts, we prefer working with normalized data rather than the original unit data. In data mining, for instance, we often normalize our data to remove units and work with standard normal scores instead. This ensures consistency and facilitates mathematical calculations, especially when dealing with distances.

Another example of data transformation is changing units of measure. For instance, if your data is in inches but you need to analyze it in centimeters, you'll need to convert the units accordingly. Additionally, data transformation can be used to address skewness in the data distribution. Various mathematical transformations, such as logarithms, can help simulate a normal distribution, which is often preferred for statistical modeling and assumptions.

Moreover, adjusting financial data is another important aspect of data transformation. Many overlook the need to adjust financial data over time, such as accounting for inflation or changes in currency value. This step ensures that financial analyses are accurate and relevant to the current economic context.

In summary, data normalization and transformation play a crucial role in statistical analyses and data modeling. These processes help standardize data, address skewness, and ensure accuracy in analytical outcomes, particularly in fields like finance and data mining.

Review Questions

1. Why do we normalize data before analysis?
2. How can transforming data, like using a log, help with skewed data?

4-4 Preprocessing text data

Preprocessing text data means modifying clean data for some purpose. Common purposes include changing order, changing case, removing special characters, putting in characters, and removing spaces. For text processing purposes, various functions are typically used. Excel offers a plethora of functions for such tasks. You can also nest functions, utilizing them within others, and explore their capabilities firsthand.

Similar functions apply if you're using R or Python. However, some may find Excel more user-friendly. Uploading data from Excel to R or Python to fix spelling errors, for instance, might seem unnecessary and cumbersome. It's often more efficient to handle such tasks directly in Excel. Coding becomes advantageous for routine tasks. If you have consistent monthly data with predictable errors, writing repeatable code in R or Python could be beneficial. But for one-time tasks like fixing a particular spelling error, using coding languages might be overkill.

Consider the nature of the task before deciding whether to use Excel or coding languages for text processing. If it's a one-off task or requires quick exploration, Excel might be the more practical choice. However, for repetitive tasks with standardized errors, coding languages offer automation benefits.

Changing order

A text preprocessing task commonly done may be to change the order of the text. The use case of this illustrated is when a name is entered in a certain way (last name, first name) and another order is desired.

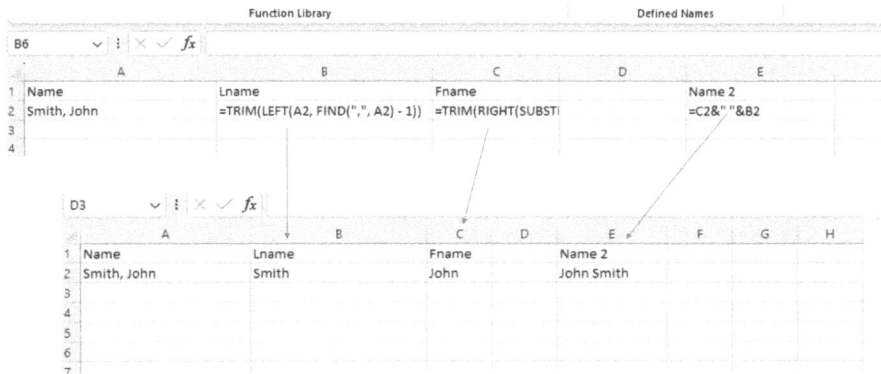

This might be necessary for formatting purposes, like when preparing mailing labels. Excel provides functions for this purpose, which may seem daunting at first glance, but with a bit of exploration, you'll find them quite intuitive to use.

Changing case

Changing cases is another text preprocessing task which is a handy feature in Excel. For instance, you might need to convert state abbreviations to uppercase. While this may seem trivial, Excel makes it easy to accomplish without diving into programming languages. Plus, with Excel, you can see your changes in real-time, allowing for a more interactive and visual approach to data manipulation. For example, to convert state abbreviations to upper-case, you can simply use the "UPPER" function, which intuitively does what its name suggests.

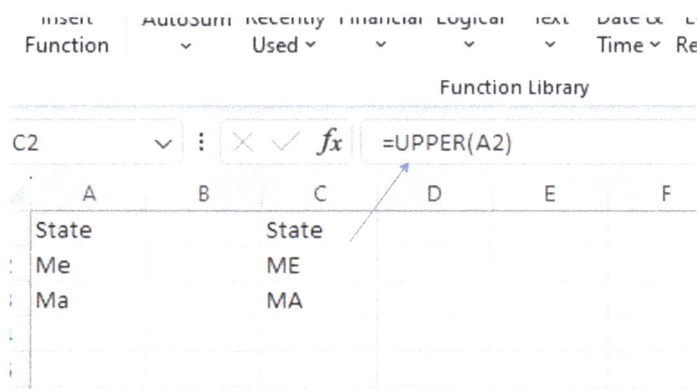

| Insert Function | Autosum ˅ | Recently Used ˅ | Financial ˅ | Logical ˅ | Text ˅ | Date & Time ˅ | Re |

Function Library

| C2 | ˅ | ⋮ | × | ✓ | fx | =UPPER(A2) |

	A	B	C	D	E	F
	State		State			
	Me		ME			
	Ma		MA			

Removing characters

Special characters can sometimes be sneaky—they might not be visible, but they could be causing alignment issues or other problems. Excel's "CLEAN" function comes in handy here. It removes non-printable characters, including those with ASCII values ranging from 0 to 31 and Unicode characters, which might be lurking in your data.

	B	C	D	E	F
	Text with linebreaks		Text no breaks		
	Hello				
	World		HelloWorld		

fx =CLEAN(B2)

CLEAN function removes non-printable characters with ASCII values from 0 to 31 (except for 9, 10, and 13), and the Unicode character 127.

Another useful tool is the "Find and Replace" feature. Whether you're dealing with a small data set or a massive one, "Find and Replace" is efficient and quick. You can swiftly locate and replace unwanted characters or strings throughout your spreadsheet, ensuring your data is clean and consistent.

Inserting characters

In addition to using functions, you can manipulate data by inserting characters where needed. For instance, if you have a five-digit zip code without dashes, you might want to insert dashes between the first and last four digits. Excel's "LEFT" function can extract the first five characters, and then the "CONCATENATE" function can combine them with a dash in between.

This formula takes the first five characters of the zip code (before the dash) using the LEFT function, adds a dash ("-"), and then takes the next four characters (after the dash) using the MID function. It concatenates these parts together using the CONCATENATE operator "&".

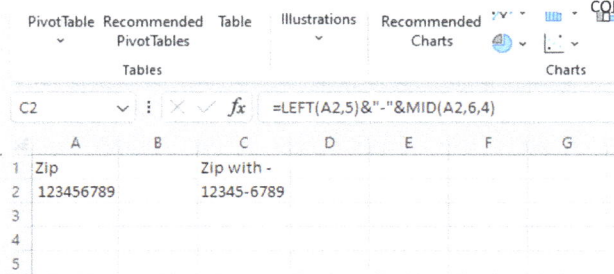

	PivotTable	Recommended PivotTables	Table	Illustrations	Recommended Charts			
		Tables				Charts		

C2			f_x	=LEFT(A2,5)&"-"&MID(A2,6,4)		

	A	B	C	D	E	F	G
1	Zip		Zip with -				
2	123456789		12345-6789				
3							
4							
5							

Remove spaces

Removing spaces from data is another common task. Excel provides the "TRIM" function for this purpose. It intelligently removes leading and trailing spaces while preserving spaces within words. The "CLEAN" function is useful for removing non-printable characters, ensuring that only valid text remains. While like "TRIM," CLEAN specifically targets non-letter ASCII characters and TRIM specifically targets spaces.

	Clipboard	⌐⌐			Font			⌐⌐	

C2		⌄	:	✕ ✓ *fx*	=TRIM(A2)	

	A	B	C	D	E
1	**Spacey text**		**Text after trim**		
2	Clean me		Clean me		
3	Clean me		Clean me		
4	Clean me		Clean me		
5					
6					
7					
8					

Split (tokenize) text data

Sometimes, you need to extract specific parts of data from a single column. This process is known as splitting or tokenizing the data. For example, you might want to extract just the subject from course codes like "MATH 106" or "MATH 206." Similarly, if you have dates with both month and year, you can split them to analyze each component separately. Splitting data becomes crucial when dealing with compound fields like addresses, where you might need to separate elements like town, state, and ZIP code for further analysis. These techniques allow for more granular analysis and organization of data.

Splitting data, sometimes referred to as tokenization, involves breaking down text into individual words or tokens. This process is essential for natural language processing and AI tasks, which are becoming increasingly relevant in our program. While we've covered some text analysis in the applied data course, there's potential for a dedicated text analysis course in the future.

In Excel, there are various text functions available for extracting and tokenizing text. The "LEFT" and "RIGHT" functions extract a specific number of characters from the beginning and end of a string, respectively. Additionally, the "MID" function can extract characters from the middle of a string.

Clipboard	⌄		Font		⌄	Alignm

C2 ⌄ : ✕ ✓ *fx* =LEFT(A2,4)

	A	B	C	D	E	F	G
	Course		Subject only				
	MATH181		MATH				
	MATH205		MATH				

Clipboard	⌄		Font		⌄

C2 ⌄ : ✕ ✓ *fx* =RIGHT(A2,3)

	A	B	C	D	E
1	Course		Number		
2	MATH181		181		
3	MATH205		205		
4					
5					

Excel's "Text to Columns" feature, found under the "Data" tab, automatically splits data based on specified delimiters, such as spaces or commas.

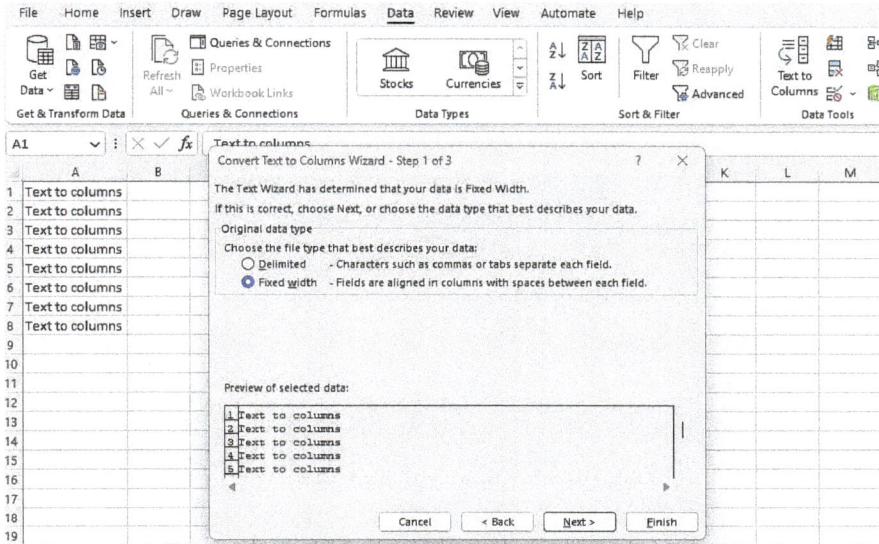

Consolidate (join) data

To modify data, you may need to consolidate or concatenate data. This involves joining multiple strings together. In Excel, the "CONCATENATE" function or "JOIN" function. Typically, "joining" tables refers to combining data from multiple tables based on common fields, while "concatenating" or "consolidating" typically involves combining fields within a single table. The terms "consolidate" and "concatenate" can be used interchangeably, both implying the merging of fields.

To consolidate fields in Excel, the "CONCATENATE" function is handy. For instance, to combine first names and last names, you can use this function to concatenate them with a space in between.

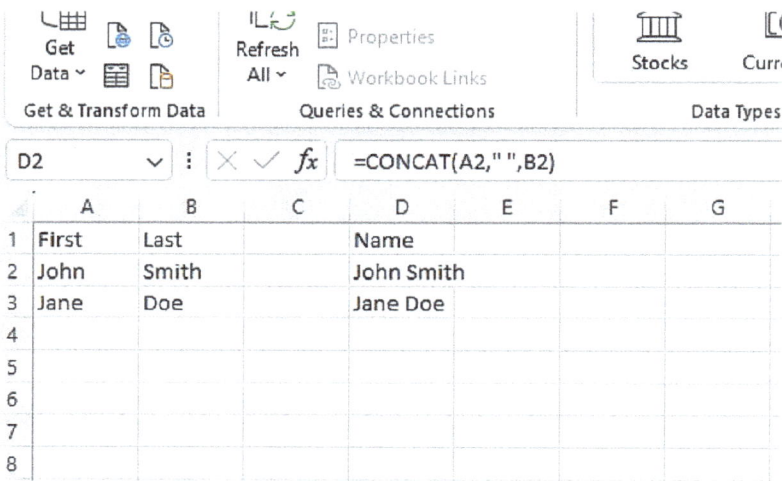

Adding a prefix to IDs can be useful for ensuring they are treated as text fields rather than numeric ones. This can be achieved by concatenating the prefix with the ID number.

Get & Transform Data	Queries & Connections	Data Types

C2	⌄ ⋮ ✕ ✓ *fx*	=CONCAT("A",A2)

◢	A	B	C	D	E	F	G
1	ID		New ID				
2		1	A1				
3		2	A2				
4		3	A3				
5							
6							
7							
8							

Review Questions

1. What is text preprocessing? Give two examples.
2. When is Excel a better choice than R or Python for text tasks?
3. Which Excel function makes text all uppercase?
4. What does the "CLEAN" function do?
5. How can you switch the order of names (last name, first name) in Excel?
6. How can you add a dash into a zip code in Excel?
7. What is the difference between "TRIM" and "CLEAN"?
8. How would you split "MATH 106" into two parts in Excel?
9. What is the difference between splitting text and joining text?
10. Why might you add a prefix to an ID number? How would you do it?

4-5 Binning data

Learning Outcomes

4-5-1 Define binning and explain its purpose in data analysis.
4-5-2 Distinguish between binning continuous and categorical data.
4-5-3 Identify potential challenges and pitfalls associated with binning.

Binning, which can also be referred to as grouping or categorizing, is a common practice used to organize data into discrete categories. In a statistics class binning is often used when teaching about creating frequency distributions. When dealing with continuous data, binning becomes necessary as you have an infinite number of possible values. By binning the data into intervals like 0 to 10, 11 to 20, and so on, we can create meaningful frequency tables.

Binning can be applied to both continuous and categorical data. It provides structure and organization, making complex datasets more manageable and interpretable. For instance, with categorical data like individual state information, grouping states into regions becomes essential for analysis. This aggregation allows for a more manageable dataset and facilitates comparisons between regions.

When binning continuous quantitative variables, it's crucial to avoid overlap between categories. Each category should be exclusive, with clear boundaries. For example, a value of 12.4 might fall into the category of 10 to less than 15, emphasizing that it's less than 15 but not including it. This ensures clarity and accuracy in the categorization process. When binning numeric data, you essentially transform it into categorical data.

For categorical data without a high number of possible values, such as gender (male, female, other, non-binary), binning may not be necessary. However, for variables like college majors with numerous subcategories (e.g., biology, nutrition, chemistry), grouping them into broader categories like "Sciences" or "Humanities" can be beneficial. The decision to bin depends not only on the number of categories but also on their distribution and significance.

Binning, however, isn't without its pitfalls. It's essential to ensure that your binning process is meaningful and well-defined. For instance, creating a category like "minority" might seem innocuous, but it lacks clarity. When binning numeric data, such as age, the intervals don't have to be uniform. For age groups, I often used categories like "kids," "young adults," "adults," and "older adults," which weren't necessarily in ten-year intervals. The key to binning is to have clarity in the categories you create. Whether it's defining what constitutes a neighborhood or specifying age groups, clarity is crucial.

Additionally, be mindful of the "other" category. While it may seem like a catch-all, it's essential to understand the frequency and distribution of data within this category to avoid losing valuable insights. In categorical data analysis, such as the CDC's chart on causes of death, where most deaths are attributed to a few common causes, it's common practice to bin or group the data. For instance, the top 10 causes are listed individually, while the rest are grouped under an "other" category. This approach makes sense when dealing with numerous less common causes, consolidating them for easier interpretation. However, the "other" category can be overly broad, obscuring specific details and warranting caution in its use.

Binned data is aggregated, resulting in the loss of granularity from the original dataset. While aggregation simplifies analysis, preserving the granular data is essential for deeper insights. Thus, it's crucial never to discard the original data.

Ultimately, whether to bin data involves judgment calls based on the data's characteristics and analytical goals. It's essential to consider the implications of binning on data interpretation and ensure that the chosen approach aligns with the analysis objectives.

Example

Data binning, also known as discretization, is a technique used to group a range of continuous values into a smaller number of "bins" or intervals. This helps simplify the analysis of data and can reveal patterns that may not be obvious when examining individual values. A simple example can be seen when working with a list of people's ages.

Suppose we have the following list of ages: 5, 12, 17, 24, 32, 45, 52, 63, and 78. Instead of treating each age separately, we can group them into meaningful categories based on age ranges. For instance, we might define the bins as follows: ages 0–12 as "Child," 13–19 as "Teenager," 20–35 as "Young Adult," 36–55 as "Adult," and 56 and older as "Senior."

Using these definitions, the ages would be classified into categories as follows: 5 and 12 would fall under "Child," 17 under "Teenager," 24 and 32 as "Young Adult," 45 and 52 as "Adult," and both 63 and 78 as "Senior."

Review Questions

1. What is binning, and why is it important when working with continuous data?
2. How does binning help organize complex datasets for easier analysis?
3. Give an example of how binning can be used with categorical data.
4. Why must the categories in binning be exclusive and clearly defined?

Chapter 5

DATA RESTRUCTURING

Data restructuring is the final tier of data wrangling. By this stage, data has been cleaned within columns, modifications and adjustments have been made, and standardization has been implemented. Now, it's time to restructure the data if necessary.

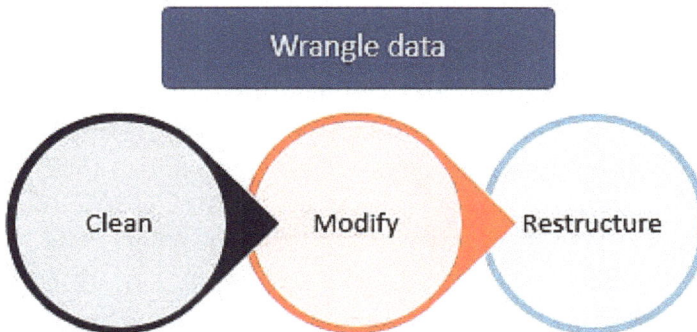

5-1 Data restructuring basics

Learning Outcomes

5-1-1 Understand the purpose of data restructuring.

So, what exactly is data restructuring? It involves changing the format of the dataset itself, often by aggregating data, sub setting, or joining datasets. Essentially, it's about modifying the organization or structure of the data. For example, you might subset a large dataset to focus on specific columns or groups, join datasets together, or create an aggregated dataset with summarized information.

Data restructuring is crucial for preparing data for analysis, including statistical modeling and visualization. It ensures that the data is in a format conducive to the specific requirements of the analysis. Different analyses require different layouts; for instance, time series analysis necessitates specific data arrangements. Repeated measures analysis, briefly touched upon in statistics, also demands data in a particular format, thus requiring restructuring. Even if you don't need to subset or aggregate data, restructuring can still make it easier to work with, especially for junior team members or students who may be handling the data.

Various tools are available for restructuring data. While Excel is commonly used, it may not be the most efficient choice for this task. Restructuring may be best achieved using SQL or a programming language like R or Python.

Prior to data restructuring, it's crucial to ensure that the data is clean and modified, as indicated in the familiar three-circle data wrangling diagram. After cleaning, restructuring can be performed based on specific needs. It's common to perform multiple restructuring iterations on the same dataset, tailoring subsets for different purposes, such as time series analysis or creating simplified versions for junior analysts.

It's essential to differentiate between data restructuring and temporary modifications like filtering and sorting. Filtering and sorting typically involve temporary adjustments for viewing purposes, whereas restructuring involves altering the dataset's organization.

Restructuring methods encompass pivoting, melting, transposing, stacking, unstacking, merging, and joining—essentially data gymnastics. These methods can be used individually or in combination, depending on the task at hand. Each method serves a different purpose, and while specifics may vary, it's essential to grasp the broader perspective of data wrangling techniques.

5-2 Modifying the data structure

Learning Outcomes

5-2-1 Understand how different software uses data table types and why it matters for analysis.

Different software allows you to change the data table type, altering its properties and behaviors.

For example, in Excel, you can easily create a table format from the date sheet. This transforms the data from a regular spreadsheet into a table with distinct properties from a regular spreadsheet, including having properties of a relational data table. Relational database tables, allowing for operations like joins, are often used in business classes.

	A	B	C	D	E	F	G	H	I	J
1	age	first_nam	vin	last_name						
2	27	Theodore	KG0TAHAI	Butler						
3	60	Kevin	XX3709LL2	Hughes						
4	38	Andrew	X6TTR34Z\	Sanders						
5	38	Victoria	0903A8V7	Cooper						
6	44	Michelle	ATZ3JW8G	Davis						
7	77	Anthony	KJUN8E6J	Hill						
8	55	Aiden	LSK636K5I	Price						
9	65	Richard	1RGBPCLC	Cook						
10	73	Justin	VGLKDZ20	Young						
11	50	Justin	EYUXFNW	Anderson						
12	28	Richard	T7Y95BH4	White						
13	22	Allison	RMFWZDY	Miller						
14	66	Erin	WE1PPFZ\	Gray						
15	55	Benjamin	SFU4MM9	Robinson						
16	19	Jeremy	UUDNWZL	Lopez						
17	58	Haley	7M53DNB	Adams						
18	47	Elizabeth	2ZFSEHFJ/	Bryant						
19	35	Matthew	T2J5U8FG(	Ward						
20	74	Charlotte	YSDYRNN!	Butler						
21	24	Hannah	XPRHZ3C9	Edwards						

Select data
range,
choose
insert table,
confirm
create table
('OK')

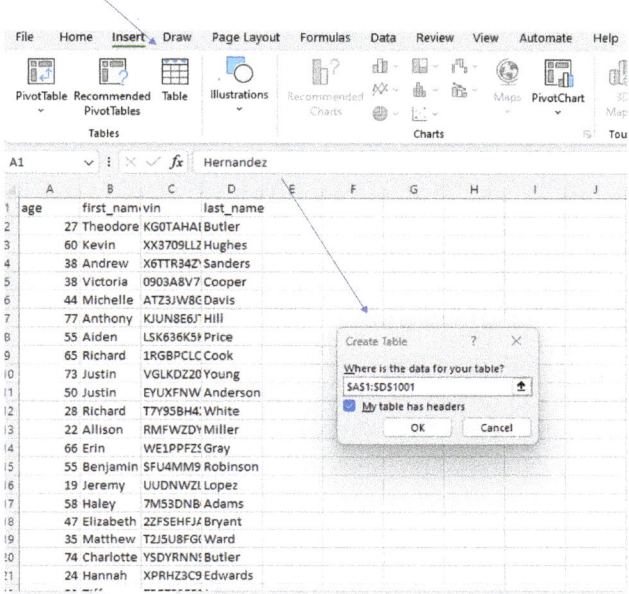

Table Name:	Summarize with PivotTable	Insert Slicer	Export	Refresh	Properties
	Remove Duplicates				Open in Browser
Table1					
Resize Table	Convert to Range				Unlink
Properties	Tools		External Table Data		

A1   ∨ : ✕ ✓ *fx*

	A	B	C	D	E	F	G	H
1	age	first_name	vin	last_name				
2	27	Theodore	KG0TAHAI	Butler				
3	60	Kevin	XX3709LLZ	Hughes				
4	38	Andrew	X6TTR34Z\	Sanders				
5	38	Victoria	0903A8V7	Cooper				
6	44	Michelle	ATZ3JW8G	Davis				
7	77	Anthony	KJUN8E6J]	Hill				
8	55	Aiden	LSK636K5F	Price				
9	65	Richard	1RGBPCLC	Cook				
10	73	Justin	VGLKDZ20	Young				
11	50	Justin	EYUXFNW	Anderson				
12	28	Richard	T7Y95BH4]	White				
13	22	Allison	RMFWZDY	Miller				
14	66	Erin	WE1PPFZ9	Gray				
15	55	Benjamin	SFU4MM9	Robinson				
16	19	Jeremy	UUDNWZL	Lopez				
17	58	Haley	7M53DNB	Adams				
18	47	Elizabeth	2ZFSEHFJ/	Bryant				

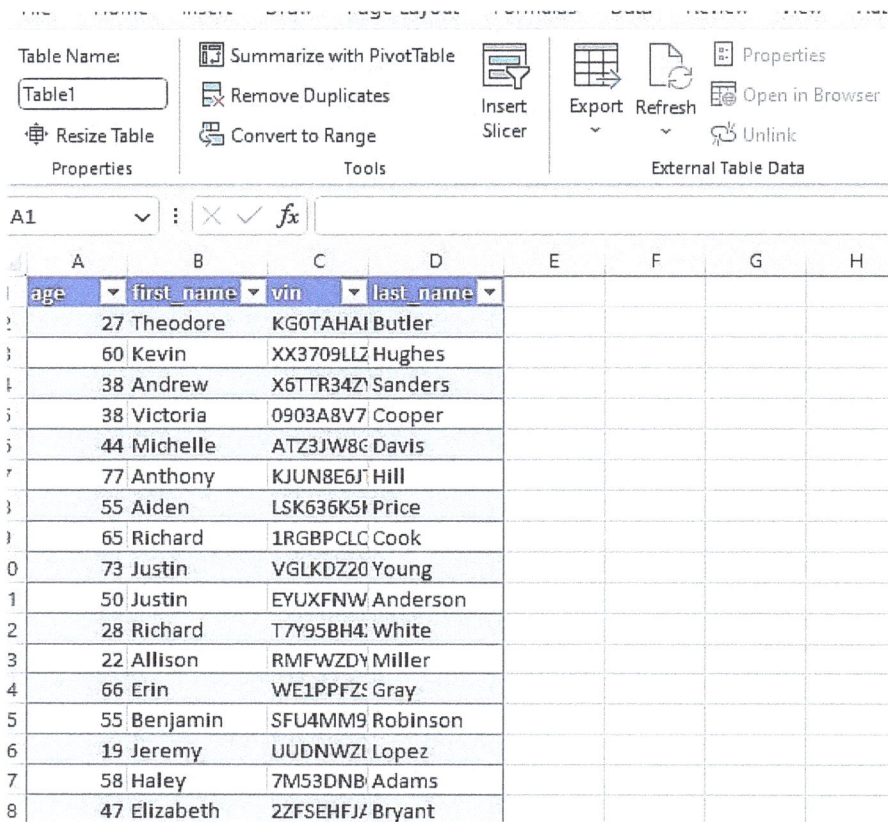

In R, the standard base package creates a data frame, while the Tidy verse package converts it into a Tibble, offering specialized functions. Base R serves as the foundation, while Tibbles are an enhanced version with additional features. Tibbles retain all data frame functionality but offer additional capabilities, requiring extra packages compared to base R. This concept aligns with object-oriented inheritance, where Tibbles build upon base R.

Review Questions

1. What's the benefit of converting a range to a table in Excel?
2. How do relational tables differ from regular spreadsheets?
3. What makes a Tibble different from a data frame in R?

5-3 Variable names and order

Learning Outcomes

5-3-1 Understand why changing variable names and order matters.

5-3-2 Know why it's important to document name changes.

Another aspect of data restructuring involves altering field attributes, including variable order. This can impact data structure, such as rearranging columns. SQL is often the preferred tool for such tasks, given its versatility and universality. SQL has been a staple in analytics since the late 1990s, providing enduring value. In contrast, tools like Python and R may evolve over time, making SQL and Excel more reliable choices. Renaming variables, for instance, is easily achieved with SQL's select statement (covered in the last section of this chapter).

Variable names may need to be changed for several reasons. Before joining data, it's crucial to ensure variable consistency, such as renaming similar ID fields. This preemptive step avoids discrepancies during data merging. If you have two fields with identical names that represent different data, it's imperative to avoid joining them inadvertently. This situation might arise due to poorly chosen names, whether by yourself or someone else. Ambiguously named fields can cause confusion and should be made more specific, especially if they need to align with certain naming standards.

Documentation becomes crucial when changing variable names to prevent misunderstandings. It's essential to notify anyone using the data about the changes and update all related documents and code snippets accordingly.

Changing variable names can introduce complications, particularly in coding environments. Any existing code referencing the old variable names would need to be updated to reflect the changes. This process can be time-consuming and prone to errors if not handled meticulously. Thus, thorough documentation and careful planning are essential when modifying variable names to avoid unnecessary headaches.

In Excel, the concept of variables and variable names isn't as prominent as in programming languages like R. Instead, columns are typically denoted by letters (e.g., Column A, Column B), and the first row often serves as headers (that are pseudo-variable names). However, it's still crucial to exercise caution when making changes in Excel, ensuring thorough documentation to avoid confusion, especially when others may access the data.

In R, creating new variables or renaming existing ones is straightforward. You can simply use the assignment operator to assign values to new variables, making the process relatively easy and intuitive.

Review Questions

1. Why is it important to rename variables before merging data?
2. What could go wrong if two columns have the same name but different data?
3. In R, how do you change a column name?

5-4 Aggregated Data

A fundamental aspect of data restructuring: creating aggregated or summary datasets. This involves consolidating data to produce summaries based on specific criteria, such as grouping all freshman students together. These aggregated datasets provide a condensed view of the data, making it easier to analyze and visualize trends. In introductory statistics courses, students often learn how to generate frequency tables and basic graphs from summarized data. Analytical tasks typically require summarized data since visualizing raw, granular data can be overwhelming and impractical. Aggregation operations like summing or averaging are applied to combine and summarize data, resulting in a new dataset distinct from the original raw data.

When you create aggregated data you now have two layers of data, there's the original granular dataset and then there's the aggregated dataset, which consolidates the data based on certain criteria. While technically you could add aggregate metrics to the original dataset, it's generally not recommended as it can clutter the dataset unnecessarily. Instead, a separate aggregated dataset is typically created for analysis, visualization, and presentation purposes. This aggregated dataset simplifies the complexity of the data, allowing for insights at a higher level, such as by class year or category.

However, it's important to exercise caution when working with aggregated data because once data is aggregated, the original details are lost. You need to retain the original source data to be able to backtrack and understand what comprises the aggregation. Without access to the granular data, it's challenging to address specific inquiries or "drill down" into the details. Some software tools offer the ability to drill down from aggregated data to its granular components, but not all programs provide this functionality.

Common aggregation operations include summing, averaging, counting, finding minimums and maximums, among others. Aggregating data requires defining groups based on specific characteristics or criteria within the dataset. It's a crucial step in data analysis, but one must always be mindful of preserving the original data details for comprehensive understanding and future reference.

Aggregating data is essential for generating insightful summaries, but it's crucial to understand that basic aggregation typically involves generating summary statistics for the entire dataset. For instance, you could calculate the average age of all students across the entire population. However, to derive more meaningful insights, you often need to group the data based on one or more categorical variables. This grouping allows for deeper analysis, such as calculating the average age of students within specific majors, enrollment status (full-time, part-time), or other categories like major and semester.

When grouping variables, you have flexibility in choosing the criteria based on which the data will be grouped. These criteria can vary widely, ranging from categorical variables like product categories or time periods (e.g., months) to numeric data that has been binned into categories. It's common to group data based on time periods, regions, product categories, or any other relevant classification that helps derive meaningful insights. The number of groups you create depends on the nature of your data and your analytical goals.

Aggregating data is used for tables and graphs and serves the purpose of

generating insightful reports and analyses, allowing businesses and organizations to extract valuable insights and make informed decisions based
on the summarized information. Aggregated data serves various purposes,
including exploratory data analysis, statistical analysis, and reducing data
complexity. When dealing with excessively large datasets, aggregation becomes essential for manageable analysis. For instance, if you have millions
of rows of data, aggregating it by year can make it more manageable while
retaining essential insights.

From a nonprogramming tool standpoint, the tool for aggregating data is
Excel pivot tables. Pivot tables excel (pun intended) in terms of easy data
restructuring to create aggregate data flexibly. They offer a user-friendly
interface for creating data summaries, even for those unfamiliar with SQL
aggregation.

Pivot tables allow users to aggregate data effortlessly by simply point-and-
clicking in Excel. This accessibility has played a significant role in Excel's
widespread adoption and its status as a perennial favorite among data analysts. An example of a pivot table is demonstrated here, showcasing the
average age within different age groups.

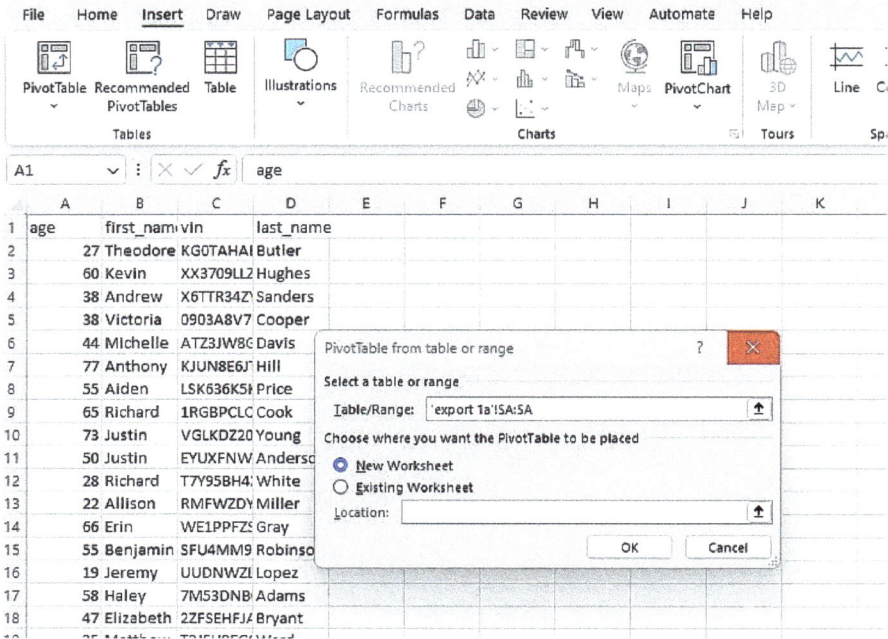

Right click on granular age to create groups, use values to compute averages

Code based aggregation of data can be performed in SQL, R and Python.

While R and Python offer their ways of performing tasks like SQL, it is usually best to prioritize learning and using SQL. Despite the allure of R and Python, SQL's longevity and widespread use make it a valuable skill in the field of data analytics. While trends may come and go, SQL remains a steadfast tool for data manipulation and analysis.

> **Review Questions**
>
> 1. What is data aggregation?
> 2. How do you aggregate data?
> 3. Why group data?
> 4. What are Pivot Tables used for?
> 5. Why keep the original data?

5-5 Subset data

> **Learning Outcomes**
>
> **5-5-1** Understand what subsetting is and how it differs from filtering.
> **5-5-2** Know how to subset data by rows or columns.
> **5-5-3** Use subsetting to focus analysis or prepare data (e.g., train/test split).
> **5-5-4** Apply subsetting to handle missing data.

Subsetting is a straightforward process that many are familiar with, but it's also a method of restructuring data. Subsetting is akin to filtering, but with a crucial difference – it's permanent. When you subset data, you're selecting specific elements based on predefined criteria. This could involve isolating segments of your dataset for focused analysis. Subsetting isn't just about filtering; it can also involve randomly sampling a subset of data, which is handy for development work, especially when dealing with extensive datasets.

The primary goal of subsetting is to narrow down your dataset to the relevant information you need. This allows you to work more efficiently without the burden of processing unnecessary data. For example, if you're analyzing sales data, you might only be interested in specific regions, time periods, product categories, or demographic segments.

Moreover, subsetting can be crucial for handling missing data in statistical analysis. By selecting only complete cases, you can sidestep the complexities associated with missing data. Additionally, in statistical modeling and data mining, creating separate test and train datasets involves subsetting. This ensures that each dataset contains complete and distinct sets of data, facilitating accurate analysis.

It's common practice to create subsets, either by columns or rows. When subsetting by columns, you're selecting specific columns of interest, such as the ones illustrated here, which may include only a few columns out of the entire dataset.

ID	RunID	PP	PH	PS	RH	RS	TimeAsof	Station	Direction	OBSSPEED	PRDSPEED	ERR
1	8 AP	5	5	15	5	1/0/1900	2	EB	61.84210587	62.31578827	0.00766
2	8 AP	5	5	15	5	1/0/1900	2	WB	54.75	56.29999924	0.028311
3	8 AP	5	5	15	5	1/0/1900	3	EB	60.5	62.65000153	0.036537
4	8 AP	5	5	15	5	1/0/1900	3	WB	56.8571434	55.8571434	0.017588
5	8 AP	5	5	15	5	1/0/1900	4	EB	65.31578827	66.66686412	0.020682
6	8 AP	5	5	15	5	1/0/1900	4	WB	63.29999924	64.15000153	0.013428
7	8 AP	5	5	15	5	1/0/1900	8	EB	61	60.95000076	0.00082
8	8 AP	5	5	15	5	1/0/1900	8	WB	62.06666565	61.43333435	0.010204
9	8 AP	5	5	15	5	1/0/1900	9	EB	60.79999924	60.94444275	0.002376
10	8 AP	5	5	15	5	1/0/1900	9	WB	64.93333435	64.62963104	0.004677
11	8 AP	5	5	15	5	1/0/1900	10	EB			
12	8 AP	5	5	15	5	1/0/1900	10	WB	60.90000163	61.625	0.011905
13	8 AP	5	5	15	5	1/0/1900	11	EB	54.37036896	57.26666641	0.05327
14	8 AP	5	5	15	5	1/0/1900	11	WB	56.85185242	59.36686489	0.044236
15	8 AP	5	5	15	5	1/0/1900	13	EB	53.33333206	56.23333359	0.064375
16	8 AP	5	5	15	5	1/0/1900	13	WB	54	56.83333206	0.052469
17	8 AP	5	5	15	5	1/0/1900	14	EB	44.13333511	47.56666565	0.077795
18	8 AP	5	5	15	5	1/0/1900	14	WB	55.13333511	56.83333206	0.030834
19	8 AP	5	5	15	5	1/0/1900	15	EB	72.19999695	71.30000305	0.012465
20	8 AP	5	5	15	5	1/0/1900	15	WB	59.70000076	61.70000076	0.033501
21	8 AP	5	5	15	5	1/0/1900	17	EB			
22	8 AP	5	5	15	5	1/0/1900	17	WB	56.09999847	54.83333206	0.022570
23	8 AP	5	5	15	5	1/0/1900	18	EB	57.20000076	55	0.038462
24	8 AP	5	5	15	5	1/0/1900	18	WB	52.73333359	51.86666489	0.016435

ID	Station	Direction	OBSSPEED	PRDSPEED
1	2	EB	61.84210587	62.31578827
2	2	WB	54.75	56.29999924
3	3	EB	60.5	62.65000153
4	3	WB	56.8571434	55.8571434
5	4	EB	65.31578827	66.66666412
6	4	WB	63.29999924	64.15000153
7	8	EB	61	60.95000076
8	8	WB	62.06666565	61.43333435
9	9	EB	60.79999924	60.94444275
10	9	WB	64.93333435	64.62963104
11	10	EB		
12	10	WB	60.90000153	61.625
13	11	EB	54.37036896	57.26666641
14	11	WB	56.85185242	59.36666489
15	13	EB	53.33333206	56.23333359
16	13	WB	54	56.83333206
17	14	EB	44.13333511	47.56666565
18	14	WB	55.13333511	56.83333206
19	15	EB	72.19999695	71.30000305
20	15	WB	59.70000076	61.70000076
21	17	EB		
22	17	WB	56.09999847	54.83333206
23	18	EB	57.20000076	55
24	18	WB	52.73333359	51.86666489

On the other hand, subsetting by rows involves filtering based on certain conditions, like the example shown here, where we're selecting rows where the "Direction" variable equals "EB."

ID	RunID	PP	PH	PS	RH	RS	TimeAsof	Station	Direction	OBSSPEED	PRDSPEED	ERR
1	8 AP		5	5	15	5	1/0/1900	2	EB	61.84210587	62.31578827	0.00766
2	8 AP		5	5	15	5	1/0/1900	2	WB	54.75	56.29999924	0.028311
3	8 AP		5	5	15	5	1/0/1900	3	EB	60.5	62.65000153	0.035637
4	8 AP		5	5	15	5	1/0/1900	3	WB	56.8571434	55.8571434	0.017588
5	8 AP		5	5	15	5	1/0/1900	4	EB	65.31578827	66.66666412	0.020682
6	8 AP		5	5	15	5	1/0/1900	4	WB	63.29999924	64.15000153	0.013428
7	8 AP		5	5	15	5	1/0/1900	8	EB	61	60.95000076	0.00082
8	8 AP		5	5	15	5	1/0/1900	8	WB	62.06666565	61.43333435	0.010204
9	8 AP		5	5	15	5	1/0/1900	9	EB	60.79999924	60.94444275	0.002376
10	8 AP		5	5	15	5	1/0/1900	9	WB	64.93333435	64.62963104	0.004677
11	8 AP		5	5	15	5	1/0/1900	10	EB			
12	8 AP		5	5	15	5	1/0/1900	10	WB	60.90000153	61.625	0.011905
13	8 AP		5	5	15	5	1/0/1900	11	EB	54.37036896	57.26666641	0.05327
14	8 AP		5	5	15	5	1/0/1900	11	WB	56.85185242	59.36666489	0.044235
15	8 AP		5	5	15	5	1/0/1900	13	EB	63.33333206	56.23333359	0.054375
16	8 AP		5	5	15	5	1/0/1900	13	WB	54	56.83333206	0.052469
17	8 AP		5	5	15	5	1/0/1900	14	EB	44.13333511	47.56666565	0.077795
18	8 AP		5	5	15	5	1/0/1900	14	WB	65.13333511	56.83333206	0.030834
19	8 AP											
20	8 AP											
21	8 AP											
22	8 AP											

ID	RunID	PP	PH	PS	RH	RS	TimeAsof	Station	Direction	OBSSPEED	PRDSPEED	ERR
1	8 AP		5	5	15	5	1/0/1900	2	EB	61.84210587	62.31578827	0.00766
3	8 AP		5	5	15	5	1/0/1900	3	EB	60.5	62.65000153	0.035537
5	8 AP		5	5	15	5	1/0/1900	4	EB	65.31578827	66.66666412	0.020682
7	8 AP		5	5	15	5	1/0/1900	8	EB	61	60.95000076	0.00082
9	8 AP		5	5	15	5	1/0/1900	9	EB	60.79999924	60.94444275	0.002376
11	8 AP		5	5	15	5	1/0/1900	10	EB			
13	8 AP		5	5	15	5	1/0/1900	11	EB	54.37036896	57.26666641	0.05327
15	8 AP		5	5	15	5	1/0/1900	13	EB	53.33333206	56.23333359	0.054375
17	8 AP		5	5	15	5	1/0/1900	14	EB	44.13333511	47.56666565	0.077795
19	8 AP		5	5	15	5	1/0/1900	15	EB	72.19999695	71.30000305	0.012465
21	8 AP		5	5	15	5	1/0/1900	17	EB			
23	8 AP		5	5	15	5	1/0/1900	18	EB	57.20000076	55	0.038462

Review Questions

1. What is subsetting in data analysis?
2. How is subsetting different from filtering?
3. Why is subsetting useful for large datasets?
4. What are two common ways to subset data?
5. How can subsetting help when dealing with missing data?

5-6 Simple restructures

Learning Outcomes

5-6-1 Know the difference between wide and long data.

5-6-2 Use pivot and melt to reshape data.

5-6-3 Transpose data by switching rows and columns.

5-6-4 Stack and unstack data for combining or separating rows.

Restructure by pivot or melt

Pivoting and melting are terms used to describe transformations between wide and long data formats. In the wide format, each row represents a single subject, while in the long format, subjects may have multiple rows due to repeated measures over time. The long format is often preferred for analyses involving repeated measures, despite its less intuitive structure.

Many statistical software, including SPSS, require data to be in a specific format for certain analyses, highlighting the importance of understanding how to transition between wide and long formats.

Melting refers to the process of converting data from wide to long format.

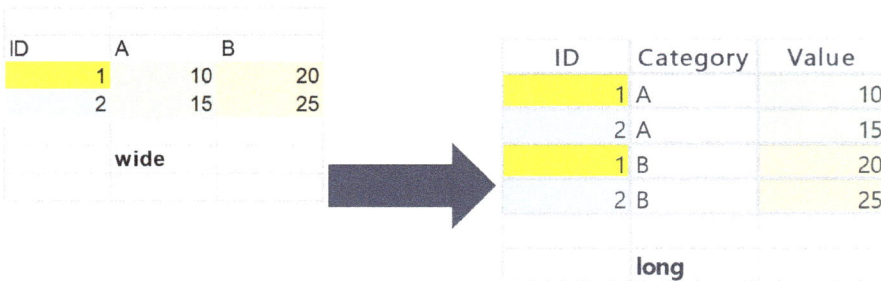

Conversely, pivoting involves transitioning from long to wide format. Although long format is more common in analytical practices, there are valid analytical reasons for opting for wide format. Hence, the term "pivot" is often used interchangeably with "long to wide" transformation.

ID	A	B
1	10	20
2	15	25
	wide	

ID	Category	Value
1	A	10
2	A	15
1	B	20
2	B	25
	long	

Restructure by transpose

Transposing is a method of restructuring data where you flip the rows and columns. While it may not be commonly used in data analytics, it's prevalent in linear algebra, which underpins many statistical concepts. Essentially, transposing involves converting columns into rows and vice versa. Excel and most programming languages have functions to transpose data tables.

ID	A	B
1	10	20
2	15	25

ID	1	2
A	10	15
B	20	25

Restructure by stack/unstack

As for stacking and unstacking, they're straightforward operations. Stacking involves vertically combining datasets, akin to stacking bricks, while unstacking is essentially subsetting. Stacking is commonly employed when consolidating data across time periods, such as combining monthly data into an annual dataset. However, it's crucial to ensure that variables are aligned correctly when stacking to avoid discrepancies.

Month	Item	N sold
January	Keys	500
January	Pens	123

Month	Item	N sold
February	Phones	590
February	Keys	600
February	Lights	283

Month	Item	N sold
March	Keys	489
March	Phones	389
March	Pens	450

Month	Item	N sold
January	Keys	500
January	Pens	123
February	Phones	590
February	Keys	600
February	Lights	283
March	Keys	489
March	Phones	389
March	Pens	450

Review Questions

1. What's the difference between wide and long formats?
2. What does melting do?
3. When do you pivot data?
4. What is transposing?
5. Why stack data?

5-7 Merging and Joining

Learning Outcomes
5-7-1 Distinguish between stacking and merging data.
5-7-2 Explain the role of key variables in merging.
5-7-3 Describe when and why to merge datasets.
5-7-4 Identify inner, left, right, and full outer joins.
5-7-5 Understand the effects of different joins on data.
5-7-6 Recognize risks like missing or duplicated data.
5-7-7 Use joins effectively and efficiently.

Merging and joining data can be a bit trickier than simple operations like stacking. While stacking involves straightforwardly combining datasets, merging and joining entail blending two datasets together, which can be more challenging. In merging, it's crucial to have a key variable, usually a unique identifier, to match records from both datasets. Relational databases often have numeric identifier variables, simplifying the merging process. However, not all datasets have such identifiers, complicating the merging task.

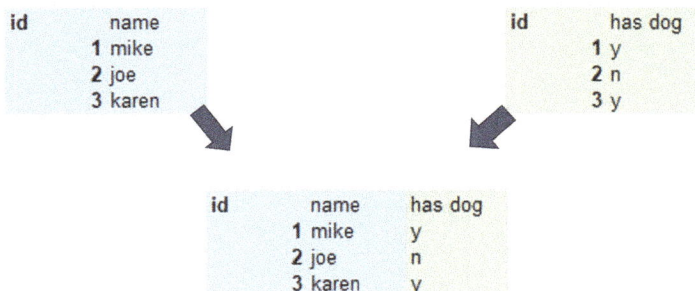

id	name
1	mike
2	joe
3	karen

id	has dog
1	y
2	n
3	y

id	name	has dog
1	mike	y
2	joe	n
3	karen	y

Merging is typically performed to consolidate related information into a single table for analytical purposes. When the data needed for analysis is spread across multiple tables, merging becomes necessary to bring everything together. This consolidation facilitates analysis by ensuring all required information is in one place.

Additionally, merging can be used to enrich datasets by incorporating supplementary information from another source. For example, adding zip code data to a dataset containing town and state information. This enrichment enhances the dataset without fundamentally altering its structure.

Another use case for merging is to address missing data by merging it with another dataset containing complementary information. While this may require some manipulation to handle missing values, merging datasets can help fill in gaps in the data.

Overall, merging and joining are essential techniques for integrating disparate datasets and preparing them for analysis, although they may require careful consideration and data manipulation to ensure successful integration.

Joins are the specific operations that merge rows from two or more tables. It's generally advisable not to attempt more than two joins simultaneously. Attempting to join four tables at once, for instance, can be overwhelming, making it difficult to monitor the process effectively. It's preferable to join two tables first, then incorporate additional tables as needed, unless there's a compelling reason not to do so. When performing joins, it's essential to closely monitor the process, keeping track of row counts and ensuring logical and coherent outcomes, avoiding messy or erroneous results.

Types of joins

There are several types of joins, each serving different purposes. The choice of join depends on the specific requirements of the task at hand. The two primary types of joins are inner joins and outer joins. An inner join combines rows that have matching values in both tables, akin to the "and" case in probability theory. In an inner join, only the intersecting rows are included, as demonstrated in the example where only IDs 1, 2, 4, and 5 appear.

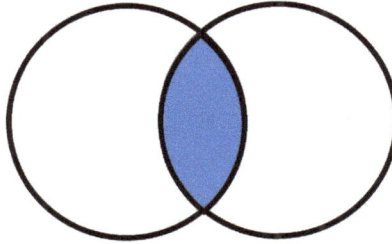

table a

id	name
1	pete
2	mack
3	nero
4	james
5	fred

table b

id	town
1	here
2	there
4	elsewhere
5	earth
7	mars

inner join of table a and b by id

id	name	town
1	pete	here
2	mack	there
4	james	elsewhere
5	fred	earth

On the other hand, an outer join includes rows from both tables, even if they don't have matching values. There are three kinds of outer joins: left, right and full.

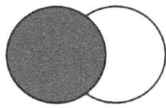

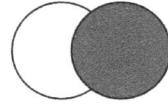

Left   Full   Right

A left join, for instance, retains all rows from the "base" table (Table A) and adds matching rows from the "additional" table (Table B). If there's no match in Table B for a row in Table A, the row remains in the result set, unlike in an inner join where it would be excluded. Left joins are commonly used to enrich data from a primary table with information from a secondary table.

table a

id	name
1	pete
2	mack
3	nero
4	james
5	fred

table b

id	town
1	here
2	there
4	elsewhere
5	earth
7	mars

left join of table a
to b by id

id	name	town
1	pete	here
2	mack	there
3	nero	
4	james	elsewhere
5	fred	earth

Similarly, right joins function similarly to left joins but with the roles reversed. However, in practice, left joins are often sufficient for most use cases, rendering right joins less common.

table a

id	name
1	pete
2	mack
3	nero
4	james
5	fred

table b

id	town
1	here
2	there
4	elsewhere
5	earth
7	mars

right join of table a
to table b by id

id	town	name
1	here	pete
2	there	mack
4	elsewhere	james
5	earth	fred
7	mars	

Full outer joins, meanwhile, combine rows from both tables, resembling the "or" case in probability theory, ensuring that all rows from both tables are included in the result set, even if there are no matching values. Beware of the term "full join" as it entails an operation that generates every possible combination, akin to a Cartesian product. For instance, if one set contains elements 1, 2, and 3, and another set contains 4 and 5, the Cartesian product would yield combinations like 1-4, 1-5, 2-4, 2-5, and so forth. While full joins are not commonly utilized, they can significantly inflate the resulting dataset, especially with larger input sets. Even a modest dataset of three rows each can explode into nine rows with a full join. Imagine the scale when dealing with thousands of rows.

Table ONE

X	A
1	a
4	d
2	b

Table TWO

X	B
2	x
3	y
5	v

X	A	X	B
1	a	2	x
1	a	3	y
1	a	5	v
4	d	2	x
4	d	3	y
4	d	5	v
2	b	2	x
2	b	3	y
2	b	5	v

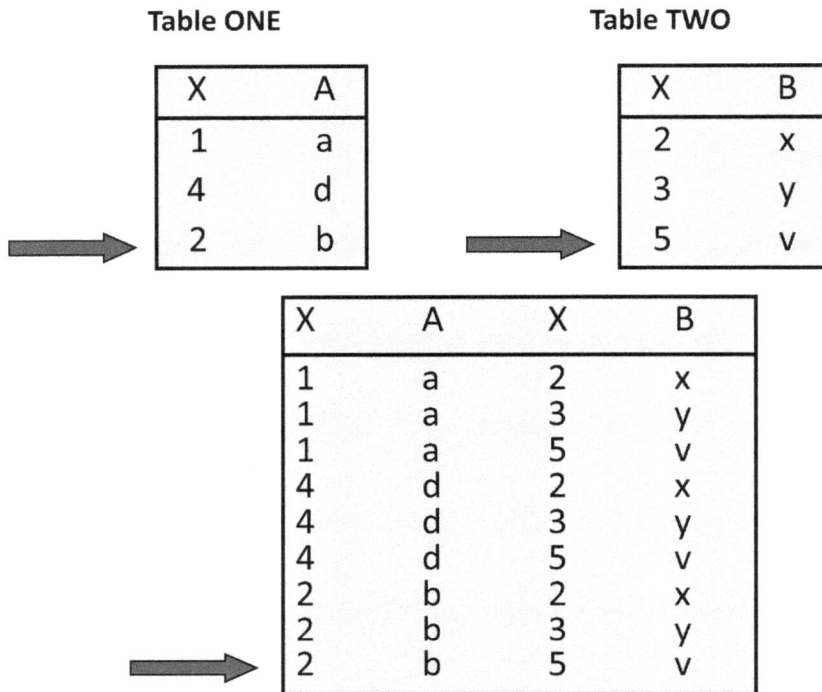

Exercise caution when performing any joins, as they can introduce various issues. Inexperienced junior analysts may inadvertently create problems, especially without proper guidance. Joining datasets can lead to missing values, especially with inner joins where unmatched data vanishes. Additionally, duplicate values may arise if one table has unique identifiers while the other has multiple occurrences. This can distort counts and analysis results, leading to confusion.

Moreover, merging datasets, especially through full joins, can strain computer resources. Even robust systems may struggle to handle the computational load imposed by extensive join operations. In some cases, it might be necessary to offload processing to more powerful machines, such as remote servers, to avoid overwhelming local resources.

In summary, while merging datasets can be a powerful tool for data analysis, it's essential to approach it with care and foresight. Understanding the nuances of different join types and their implications is crucial for producing accurate and meaningful results without overburdening computational resources.

Review Questions

1. Distinguish between stacking and merging data.
2. Explain the role of key variables in merging.
3. Describe when and why to merge datasets.
4. Identify inner, left, right, and full outer joins.
5. Understand the effects of different joins on data.
6. Recognize risks like missing or duplicated data.
7. Use joins effectively and efficiently.

5-8 VLOOKUP

Learning Outcomes

5-8-1 Use VLOOKUP to link data from different tables.
5-8-2 Understand its limitations compared to SQL.

Essentially, VLOOKUP is an Excel function that allows you to match data from one table to another based on a common identifier, such as an ID. While convenient for basic data linkage tasks, it's not a replacement for mastering SQL and performing more sophisticated joins.

For example, suppose you have a dataset with IDs, names, and ages, and you want to incorporate salary data from another table. Using VLOOKUP, you can retrieve the salary associated with each ID by specifying the lookup parameters. While VLOOKUP works within the same workbook, cross-workbook usage may be possible but not recommended due to potential complications.

K15					

	A	B	C	D	E	F	G
	ID	Name	Age				
	1 John		25				
	2 Alice		30				
	3 Bob		35				
	4 Mary		40				

Before merge | Data to merge | After merge

Clipboard	⌐|	Font		⌐|	Alignment		⌐|

A6 | ∨ | ⋮ | × ✓ ƒx |

	A	B	C	D	E	F	G	H
1	**ID**	**Salary**						
2	1	50000						
3	2	60000						
4	3	70000						
5	4	80000						
6								
7								
8								
9								
10								
11								
12								
13								
14								
15								
16								
17								
18								
19								
20								
21								

< > | Before merge | **Data to merge** | After merge | +

Clipboard ⬎			Font	⬎		Alignment	⬎	Numb

| D2 | ∨ | : | × | ✓ | *fx* | =VLOOKUP(A2,'Data to merge'!A2:B5,2,FALSE} |

	A	B	C	D	E	F	G	H	I
1	ID	Name	Age	Salary					
2	1	John	25	50000					
3	2	Alice	30	60000					
4	3	Bob	35	70000					
5	4	Mary	40	80000					
6									
7									
8									
9									
10									
11									
12									
13									
14									
15									
16									
17									
18									
19									
20									
21									

< >   Before merge | Data to merge | **After merge** | +

Ready

VLOOKUP serves as a handy Excel tool for simple data integration tasks, allowing for easy monitoring and validation through methods like pivot tables. However, it lacks the robustness and flexibility of SQL joins for complex data manipulation and analysis. Therefore, while understanding VLOOKUP is beneficial for Excel users, it should be seen as a supplementary technique rather than a comprehensive solution for data joining.

5-9 SQL for data restructuring

Learning Outcomes

5-9-1 Use SELECT to retrieve and rearrange data columns.
5-9-2 Create new tables with CREATE TABLE AS SELECT.
5-9-3 Filter and group data using WHERE, GROUP BY, and HAVING.
5-9-4 Join tables using JOIN statements.

SQL, or Structured Query Language, has been around for quite some time. SQL emerged alongside relational databases and is the standard language for querying and manipulating data. SQL's versatility is remarkable, and while it may have slight variations in implementation across different platforms like SAS and R, the core principles remain consistent. It's renowned for its simplicity and efficiency, especially when compared to other methods of data manipulation. Now, SQL isn't just for querying data; it's also capable of database management tasks like creating tables and inserting data. This aspect is typically associated with backend database systems like Microsoft SQL Server. Here though the interest is in the use of SQL for analytics.

Learning SQL offers numerous advantages. It's a classic tool that's universally recognized and used across various industries. Additionally, SQL queries are often more efficient, making them ideal for handling large datasets. Many analytics programs, such as SAS, incorporate SQL functionalities, further emphasizing its importance in the field.

So, let's delve into SQL and see how it can streamline our data restructuring processes. With its straightforward syntax and powerful querying capabilities, SQL is an indispensable tool for any data analyst or scientist. Let's dive in and explore its potential.

SELECT statement

The fundamental query in SQL is the SELECT query, which is incredibly powerful. Most SQL operations revolve around this query. A simple SELECT query retrieves data from a table using syntax like SELECT asterisk FROM table_name, where the asterisk denotes all columns.

SELECT * FROM table_name

However, using SELECT asterick is non-selective and often results in pulling more data than necessary. To retrieve specific columns, we specify them in the SELECT statement, like SELECT column2, column1. SQL makes it easy to rearrange column order effortlessly.

Rearranging or reordering columns in SQL is straightforward, all you need to do is specify the desired order in the SELECT statement, and SQL will retrieve them accordingly. This is much simpler than manually rearranging columns in Excel, which can be a nightmare of copying, pasting, and rearranging.

SELECT col2, col1 FROM table_name

CREATE TABLE

If you want to create a new table, the SELECT statement alone won't suffice—it's purely for selecting and displaying data. To create a table, you need to use the CREATE TABLE AS SELECT statement. This command will create a new table with the selected columns in the specified order.

CREATE TABLE new_table_name AS SELECT column1, column2 FROM existing_table_name

WHERE

Additionally, SQL allows you to apply conditions to your queries using the WHERE clause. This enables you to select only the data that meets specific criteria. While the syntax may vary slightly between SQL implementations (like SAS SQL and R SQL), the basic logic remains the same. For instance, you can use a WHERE clause to filter data based on conditions like "year equals 2024." Remember, if you want to store the results in a new table, you'll need to use the CREATE TABLE command.

SELECT * FROM table_name WHERE condition

GROUP BY

When it comes to aggregating data, you're essentially condensing your dataset based on certain criteria using the GROUP BY clause. Instead of retaining the original data with its original number of rows, the result will be grouped by a specific column, such as student level (freshman, sophomore, junior, senior). For example, if you start with 500 rows in your original dataset, you'll get four rows back when you count by student level, each row representing the count of freshmen, sophomores, juniors, and seniors. The COUNT function is an example of an aggregate function used in this context.

SELECT column1, COUNT(*) FROM table_name GROUP BY column1 undefined

HAVING

Understanding the difference between the HAVING and WHERE clauses can be a bit tricky. The WHERE clause is used when you're not performing a grouping operation, whereas the HAVING clause applies conditions to the result of a GROUP BY operation. For instance, HAVING is used to specify additional conditions for the grouped data, such as requiring the count to be greater than 10.

SELECT column1, COUNT() *FROM table_name GROUP BY column1 HAVING COUNT() > 10;*

135

ORDER BY

To sort your data, you use the ORDER BY clause, which allows you to specify the column by which you want to order the result set, as well as whether it should be in ascending or descending order.

SELECT column1, column2 FROM table_name ORDER BY column1 ASC

JOINS

One of SQL's strengths lies in its ability to perform mergers and joins efficiently. Joining tables in SQL is straightforward—you simply specify the tables you want to join and the condition for the join using the ON clause. SQL is widely regarded as the best tool for performing join operations.

SELECT * FROM table1 JOIN table2 ON table1.column = table2.column

SQL's versatility and simplicity make it a powerful tool for data manipulation and analysis. It's universally recognized and widely used across different platforms. Despite slight differences in syntax between SQL implementations, its fundamental principles remain consistent. This simplicity and consistency contribute to SQL's popularity and utility in various data-related tasks. In SQL, you have the flexibility to perform various operations efficiently. For example, you can use the SELECT statement to fetch specific data, and the ORDER BY clause to sort it according to your requirements. You can even combine multiple sorting criteria for more precise results.

SQL is incredibly versatile and powerful. It's applicable across various platforms, making it a universal tool for data manipulation and analysis. For instance, you can perform a wide range of operations with SQL, such as selecting data, ordering it in ascending or descending order, or even performing complex sorting based on multiple criteria like age and score. It is better to learn SQL than do SQL equivalent work in a specific language such as Python as Python's capabilities are limited to Python environments, whereas SQL can be used in any database system.

Review Questions

1. What does the SELECT statement do in SQL?
2. How can you create a new table from selected data?
3. What's the difference between WHERE and HAVING?
4. Write a basic JOIN statement to combine two tables.

www.ingramcontent.com/pod-product-compliance
Lightning Source LLC
Chambersburg PA
CBHW051908210326
41597CB00033B/6067